Harold Newton

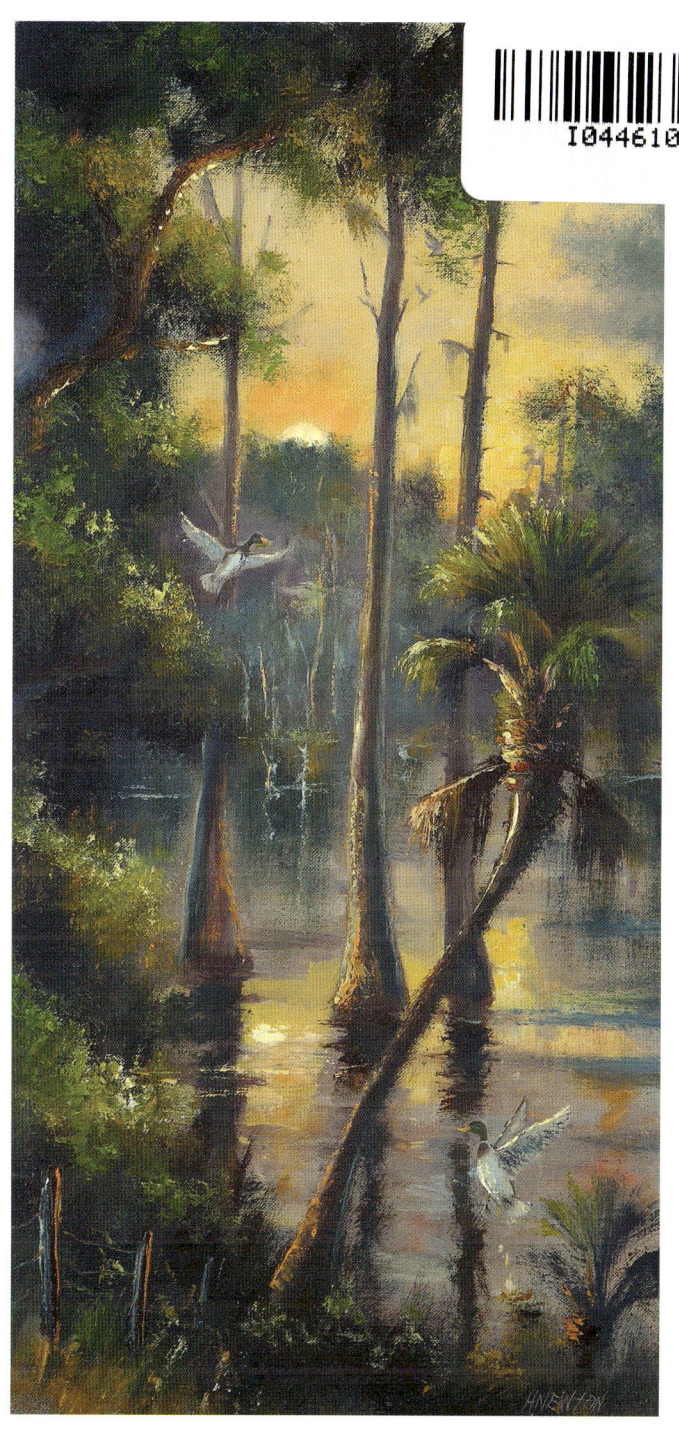

UNIVERSITY PRESS OF FLORIDA

Florida A&M University, Tallahassee
Florida Atlantic University, Boca Raton
Florida Gulf Coast University, Ft. Myers
Florida International University, Miami
Florida State University, Tallahassee
New College of Florida, Sarasota
University of Central Florida, Orlando
University of Florida, Gainesville
University of North Florida, Jacksonville
University of South Florida, Tampa
University of West Florida, Pensacola

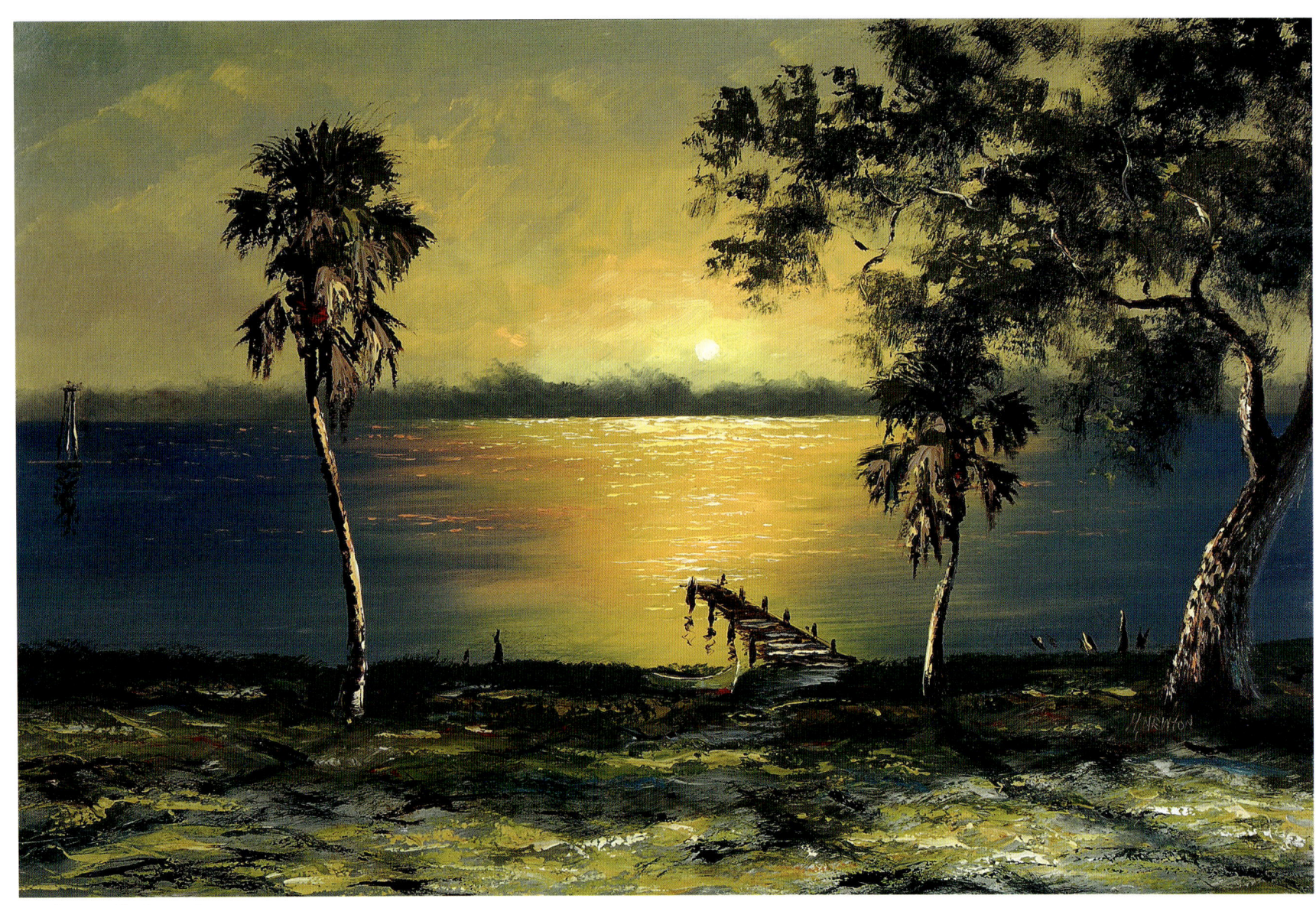

23⅝" × 35¼" oil on Masonite.

GARY MONROE

Harold Newton

The Original Highwayman

University Press of Florida

Gainesville · Tallahassee · Tampa · Boca Raton

Pensacola · Orlando · Miami · Jacksonville · Ft. Myers · Sarasota

Publication of this book was made possible through the generous support and enduring vision of Anne Frasor and Scott Schlesinger.

First cloth printing, 2007
First paperback printing, 2018

27 26 25 24 23 22   7 6 5 4 3 2

Library of Congress Cataloging-in-Publication Data
Monroe, Gary.
Harold Newton: the original Highwayman / Gary Monroe.
p. cm.
ISBN-13: 978-0-8130-3042-5 (cloth : alk. paper)
ISBN-13: 978-0-8130-6411-6 (pbk.)
1. Newton, Harold, 1934–1994. 2. African American painters—Florida.
3. Landscape in art. I. Newton, Harold, 1934–1994. II. Title.
ND237.N4875M66   2007
759.139-dc22   2006029972

The University Press of Florida is the scholarly publishing agency for the State University System of Florida, comprising Florida A&M University, Florida Atlantic University, Florida Gulf Coast University, Florida International University, Florida State University, New College of Florida, University of Central Florida, University of Florida, University of North Florida, University of South Florida, and University of West Florida.

University Press of Florida
2046 NE Waldo Road
Suite 2100
Gainesville, FL 32609
http://upress.ufl.edu

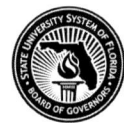

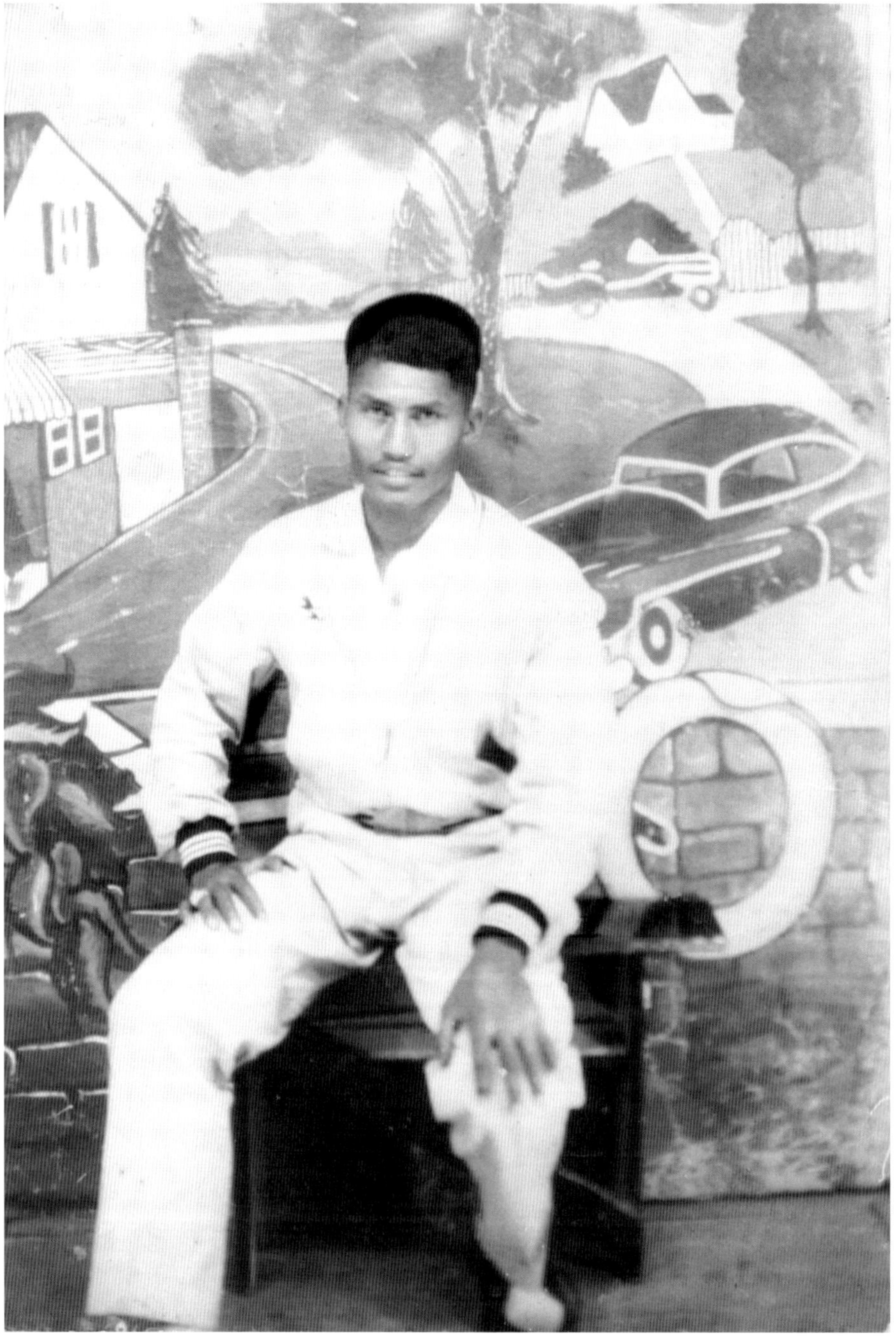

I became interested in the Highwaymen early in 1997, attracted to the paintings made by these most unlikely of artists who created a visual legacy and established a fresh aesthetic, without consciously trying to do either. Being a native Floridian, I was curious and drawn in. My initial attraction was based on Alfred Hair's fast-painting imagery, and *The Highwaymen: Florida's African-American Landscape Painters* is largely an homage to Alfred Hair's art and legacy, which includes empowering the other disenfranchised young people whose futures seemed limited by society. I increasingly appreciated the aesthetic, as their fast paintings were somehow synonymous with my own camerawork.

I am a photographer, and this midcareer tangent into the world of writing was meant to revitalize my ideas and myself or, more aptly, to ensure my maintaining photographic relevancy and vitality. Too many of my teachers, friends, and mentors burned out or gave up during midlife, as if their artistic careers were over, that there was nothing more to discover. There's nothing else I want to do, no other way I'd prefer spending my time than photographing. I am photographing with renewed energy and maybe even greater insight. Still, at times I thought that I should have bought the proverbial red Porsche.

The phone call I received early one Sunday morning in the winter of 1999, while I was researching *The Highwaymen* (UPF, 2001), was alarming. A stranger asked abruptly, before introducing himself, "Who are you to write a book about the Highwaymen?" The only logical response was "Huh?" It beat alternative responses, anyway. That was the start of a good friendship between Tim Jacobs and me.

The Highwaymen's playing field was new then. The facts of the story were sketchy at best but nevertheless widely accepted. There was no critical discussion about the artwork; nostalgia spurred interest in the paintings. I saw it as my goal to research the Highwaymen's past because I sensed that this story, possibly the last great untold tale of modern Florida (pardon my hyperbole), needed the facts sorted and interpreted for genuine appreciation of the artwork.

Tim is, to be sure, the Highwaymen's most vocal enthusiast. Upon badgering me, and maybe a tad frustrated by not engaging me in an argument, he asked if I would come to his house the next Sunday to meet a group of collectors. They were coming to pick up their paintings, which had been loaned for a Highwaymen exhibition. I think that the invitation was really a summons.

A glutton for punishment, I accepted. I stopped en route, bought a dozen bagels and cream cheese, and knocked on his door. Ed Volinnino, Henry Bosma, Mike Griffin, and Bob Hommel greeted me with indifference. Tim, on the other hand, grilled me before soon mellowing.

I think I passed the test, but there were a few moments: When I estimated the number of Highwaymen paintings to be in the range of 50,000, Tim blurted out, "Try 200,000." I asked him to do the math, and he did it fairly convincingly. Tim estimates that Harold Newton alone produced 40,000 paintings. His claim is based on the assumption that the artist completed four paintings daily, five days a week, for forty years. We don't know how many paintings Newton produced. But my research puts the number at less than 40,000. Some estimates place the number at half that and more conservative ones at almost half again. Tim's exuberance is understandable if not irrational, although he holds to it with the same vigor with which he has built a major collection.

He later told me that collectors of Highwaymen art will invariably gravitate toward collecting Harold Newton's paintings and relegate most of the others' paintings to the backs of their closets. Popular tastes confirm this to be the case. But each of the artists made paintings that mattered. Highwaymen art is of a different genus, requiring differing criteria for appreciation. Given this—and since Tim did buy a Porsche—he might have an inside track on the number of paintings produced, too. But the bottom line surely belongs to Lemuel Newton: "There's got to be a lot of 'em."

While we were sitting around Tim's dining room table, the bagels gone and schmears of cream cheese on paper napkins crumpled and scattered about, as I was going into a near-academic explication of the Highwaymen phenomenon and praising Alfred Hair for achieving the unimaginable socially, artistically, and effortlessly, Mike stopped me. He said: "You got it all wrong. You should title your book 'Harold Newton and His Followers.'" I understood and said, "That's another book."

This is it.

ACKNOWLEDGMENTS

I would be most remiss if I didn't begin by expressing appreciation for the support I have received from my wife, Teresa, and our children, Mathew and Jessica. My heart is always at home, even though I am not.

Scott Schlesinger furnished subvention funds for this book and has been unequivocally supportive throughout my research and writing.

Margie Miller edited my manuscript before I submitted it to the university press, and I am grateful for her insight and good taste. This book would be less thorough had Geoff Cook, Kevin Doty, Scott Schlesinger, and Pam Cooper, among others, not helped me along the way.

I made the best of choices when I decided to have Booth Studio of Sarasota photograph the paintings for reproduction in this book. The consternation from some of the lenders about the day trip to our state's west coast (most live on the east coast) turned to elation when they saw the quality of match-prints Booth Studio provided via Coastal Printing. Christine Alexander oversaw the production, and she made appeasing a lot of collectors and coordinating other professionals involved with the book seem easy. Eric Schumacher photographed the artwork from which Alan Murphy processed enviable digital files.

University Press of Florida's director, Meredith Babb, has long had faith in me, and for this I am thankful. Production manager Lynn Werts worked diligently, exploring new possibilities to ensure the fidelity of the paintings reproduced in this book. Larry Leshan took a personal interest in designing another Highwaymen book, and Gillian Hillis made sense of my text.

Kent Sharples, president of Daytona Beach Community College, has extended professional courtesies to me that reinforce my commitment to higher education. My colleagues Dan Biferie, Patrick Van Dusen, and Eric Breitenbach are always supportive, and for their friendship I am fortunate.

Those who shared their memories, giving freely of their time and knowledge, deserve recognition. These people informed my telling of Harold Newton's story; they invariably shaped the essay and are referenced in the text. I didn't take lightly my characterizations of those who knew Harold intimately. He was loved, and I apologize should I not please everyone. Harold lived richly and wove a complex fabric that expressed this. I did my best to lay it out evenly.

As was the case with *The Highwaymen*, there was virtually no credible source material about the artist for this book. Although almost everyone I approached was enthusiastic in their desire to help me understand Harold Newton, a few chose not to participate. Hence the perspective I use, largely based on his widow Dorothy's account, may not satisfy all his family members, but I believe that I tell the story accurately. For what it is worth, four people told me that Harold had a favorite brand of beer: Old Milwaukee, Budweiser, Schlitz, and Miller. As Pam Cooper, supervisor of the Archive Center at Indian River County Main Library, said, "It is difficult to interpret history."

Lastly, without the passionate collecting of Harold Newton's paintings by those listed, who lent their paintings for reproduction herein, this book could not have taken form:

Henry and Julia Bosma
Geoff and Patti Cook
Tim and Eileen Jacobs
Roger and Dawn Lightle
Philip and Shanon Materio
Tom and Gwen Mayes

Jorge and Pam Oliver
Jonathan and Eileen Otto
Cathy Padgett
Chris Roesner and Terry Green
Scott Schlesinger
Todd and Lisa South

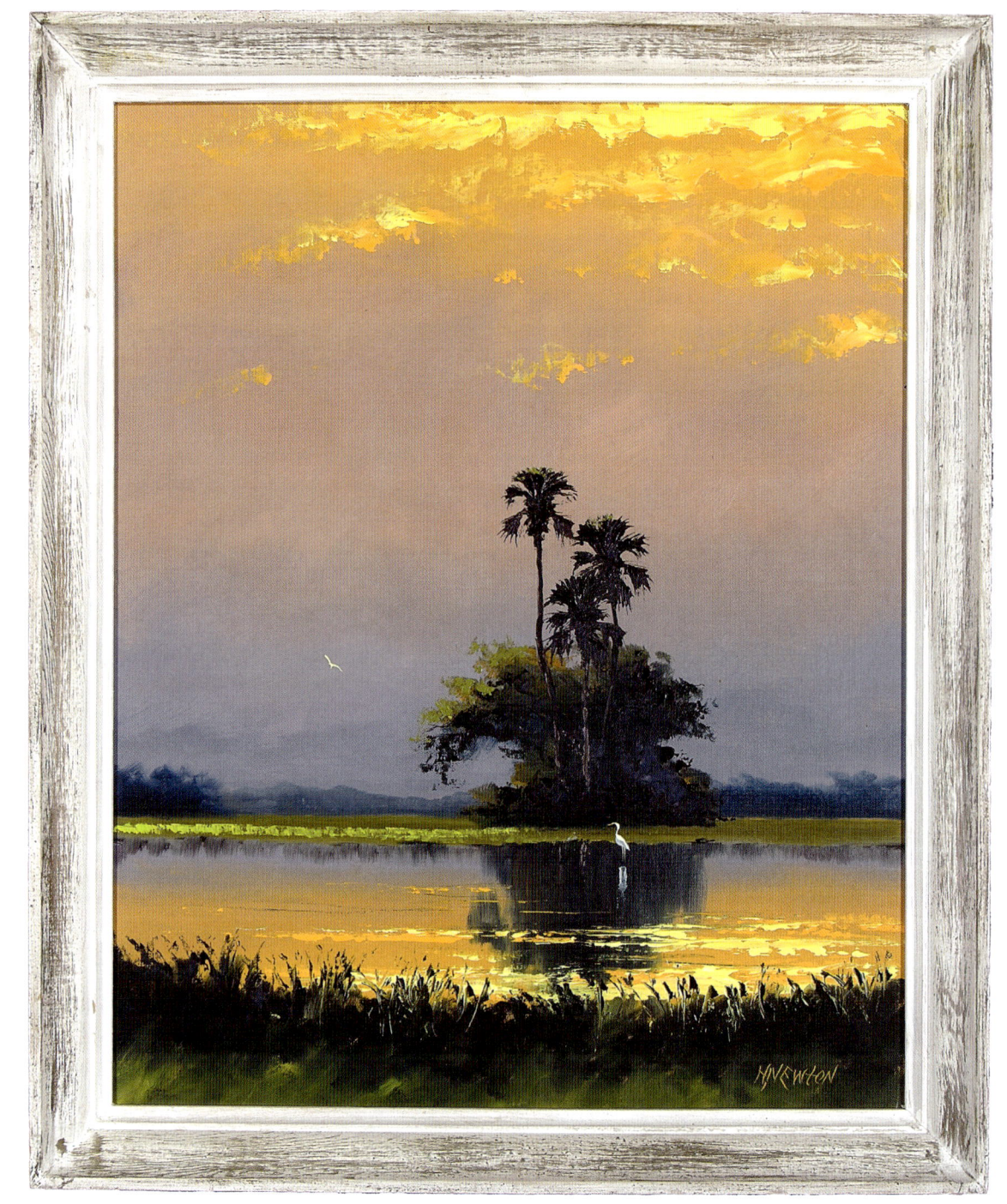

The Landscape of Desire

For everything that lives is holy, life delights in life.
WILLIAM BLAKE

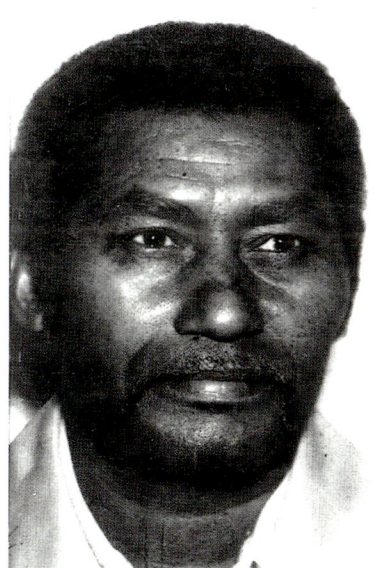

Harold Newton stood apart from the collective of African-American artists whose paintings, beginning in the late 1950s, seemed to appear out of nowhere in Florida homes and offices and spontaneously to be everywhere, as if they had always been there. These paintings symbolized how the American Dream was realized in the Sunshine State. The peninsula was still foreign and mysterious. Florida was seen as paradise. By necessity, the artists worked in near-anonymity.

The Jim Crow laws that cloaked segregation under the banner of progressive change and separate-but-equal faux integration were not deterrents to these young artists. They made their way with ease up and down the coast from their Fort Pierce area homes, determined to beat the odds by overcoming what appeared to be their social destiny—lives supported by manual labor. Rather than pick oranges and pull beans in the nearby fields, they painted prodigiously. This was a flight of fancy that would take them far and away from their apparent fate.

Without galleries or even studios, the artists stowed their paintings in their cars for day trips, selling them in towns from Daytona Beach down to Fort Lauderdale and inland, around Lake Okeechobee. Florida was booming along the Atlantic seaboard with postwar families starting afresh. The Eisenhower years were optimistic. America's vitality was echoed in Florida's landscape and was further intensified by the way these artists portrayed the verdant environs and dramatic skies.

Florida's weather was revelatory to northerners. Jet travel, interstate systems, mosquito control, and air conditioning were new, and they made the seemingly distant state increasingly accessible and desirable. Affordability, complemented by a strong economy, made Florida even more alluring. Tourism flourished along with outdoor recreation. Swaying palm trees along the coast appeared like exotic hula dancers. Although the first few feet of their trunks were often painted white as a means to repel tree-infesting insects, colored floodlights illuminated them for pure whimsy. These dreamy hues beckoned vacationers. Florida became a magnet for people with new hopes and dreams.

People were hungry for artistic scenery that was devoid of human intervention. They could feel connected to artwork with imagery resonating a sense of divinity. These new paintings seemed to quell emotional longings created by an increasingly fast-paced world. The artists gladly fed this demand, while gaining respect and making money. Financial gain motivated them; they were pulling in more cash than they could have imagined. The challenge of acquiring wealth made painting a pleasure as they showered the state with their glowing, if not transcendent, images.

Harold Newton took to the streets in 1954 to sell his paintings. By the mid-1960s, he had at least two dozen followers. But no one could depict Florida's light with the same veracity as Newton did. The sensational fleeting colors of the sunsets were lost to them. They only acknowledged this transitory light metaphorically, whereas Newton mixed pigments that actually captured the piqued and nuanced hues.

Alfred Hair was the most notable artist to come along after Newton. While in high school, Hair began taking painting lessons from the established regionalist A. E. "Bean" Backus. Hair knew that he wasn't likely to gain the acceptance that Backus, a white man, enjoyed. Having a studio and gallery representation wasn't in his cards. For Hair, painting was a ticket to ride. Money was the way out of "Blacktown." Soon the very charismatic Hair attracted other aspiring painters.

Instead of utilizing Backus's classical approach, which required exactitude and time, Hair painted fast. By creating many paintings in the same time that it took Backus to make one conventional painting and by charging a fraction of the price for each, Hair and his fellow painters earned the same amount of money, especially if they sold the paintings rapidly. And so they did: they sold them before the oils had time to dry.

Hair and those who followed him capitalized on Newton's door-to-door merchandising to sate an endless clientele. These patrons weren't likely to spend a week's salary or more for a Backus painting when they could have a reasonable facsimile—a hybrid—for relatively little. The artists' marketing strategy worked. The painters were well remunerated as they brightened countless lives and decorated numerous walls of homes and offices for more than twenty-five years. A decade later, this seemingly clandestine, loosely associated group of unlikely artists was called the "Highwaymen."

The art that emerged from the Hudson River School, in the 1830s, gave rise to American landscape painting. This imagery glorified the wonders of nature and was soon enhanced by the Luminists' poetic treatment. Man was seen as small in relation to God's Creation, but not insignificant. Rather, the individual was symbolized within a cosmology that transformed one in accord with nineteenth-century romanticism. Man ultimately was the point. Although the genre assumed a less humble attitude with the advent of Impressionism, the tradition maintained its spiritual underpinnings.

Backus had the knack, with dynamic compositions and puffy clouds, to make those who are so susceptible absolutely weak in the knees. He made the viewer feel as if he were part of the picture, completely awestruck by God's divine hand. However, if the viewer did feel like an outsider looking in, he knew that deliverance was a real possibility. Backus's paintings were objects to be adored; he was, after all, considered to be a fine artist.

As outsiders looking in, the young black artists wouldn't be as likely to objectify the land in which they lived and worked in quite the same mannered way as would trained artists who made the place seem less important than the art. Their bare-bones renditions encouraged people to look at tangled vegetation as an attainable paradise. With the veneer of civilization stripped away, viewers could experience life in all its primal glory, at least vicariously, from the comfort of their living room.

Backus provided the high-water mark, and Newton made it accessible to the then-fledgling area painters. Fast painting defined them, giving credence to Sam Newton's position of disavowing any association with the Highwaymen, for himself and his brothers Lemuel and Harold. Indeed, compared with Harold, whose paintings weren't rushed and were considerably more refined, the others' paintings may have looked inferior, and by traditional standards they were. Harold created paintings more formally astute than those by any of the other Highwaymen. Their common strength was their unconventional approach.

Some of the painters took their time with their art, but it was speed that led to Alfred Hair's distinctive imagery. His broad and exuberant brushstrokes came from the shoulder, without a care in the world, and his painterly style reflected the turbulent 1960s, whereas Harold Newton's style masked it beautifully with his fine handiwork. He achieved universal appeal with images in heavenly concert. Newton's paintings provided the measure of excellence that the other artists could only dream of achieving. They were awed by his work. Even Backus had, on occasion, acknowledged Newton's great talent. Clearly, the Highwaymen didn't know the virtues of their own paintings.

Newton's pictures lulled the masses into their dream worlds, overshadowing the fleeting informality of the quintessential Highwaymen paintings. The magic of their art was in that style, and that style was like the land itself—evocative, furtive, and unpredictable, a place for those with a pioneering spirit. Newton provided a sense of permanence and even security in contrast to Hair's temporal world.

Newton embodied the enigmatic quality that marks the romantic notion of artists. His exemplary skill provides the missing link, bridging the high and popular arts. He is central to understanding the phenomenon of landscape painting that emerged from the Indian River area and to assessing broader aesthetic issues especially as they relate to Florida as a mythic place. Newton captured not only the meaning of the semitropics but also the aura of the artiste.

During the past decade, the Highwaymen have burst onto the scene and into public awareness with a zeal that would make the best Madison Avenue ad executives envious. But as the dust settles, it becomes increasingly clear that this phenomenal accomplishment would not have happened had it not been for Harold Newton. The story would have unfolded differently and probably would have been remembered as a wonderful folk tale about how Alfred Hair empowered other young African-Americans before his death at age twenty-nine. It could have concluded with his enabling his friends and family to escape the bleak lives they faced at home and with the paintings seen more as artifacts than as art.

Harold Newton's implacably beautiful scenes became insignias of rank for the other painters as well as for Floridians. He was the perfect ambassador for the multitudes who were making Florida home. His paintings brought nature indoors. They became extensions of the outdoors, suggesting to people that by hanging one of these landscapes on a wall, they could overcome modernity's alienation from nature. While Florida as a place of rejuvenation was settled and later bulldozed out of existence, development of the land fueled the interest in and renaissance of Highwaymen art.

Defining aesthetics as the evolution of art suggests that our shared notion of beauty and meaning is fluid and ever-changing. Museum culture, since the Highwaymen emerged, has been based largely on this view of a rapidly evolving visual language, as art became primarily about art. It became increasingly idea-driven to the point of not looking like art, at least not to the layperson, for whom such art was not made or readily available. In recent times, postmodern aesthetics has recast art to be even more esoteric, less about imagery and in favor of theory, something akin to art eating itself. Critique and parody have ruled, along with intellectual posits ranging from issues of authenticity to questions of representation.

Although uninitiated in the ways of the fine arts, the people who gravitated to the Highwaymen had little doubt about or much interest in issues of aesthetics, especially as they related to authenticity and representation. They wanted pictures that looked like their surroundings, and it was even more desirable if these images were idealized enough to lift their spirits. They wanted pictures that commemorated their time and place in history. It was even better yet if they were affordable. At about twenty-five dollars each, including a frame, they were.

Newton and the other artists largely appropriated Backus's memorable and marketable images during their nascent trials. This included flowers and short-lived scenes of Jamaica, where the artist had a studio-retreat. As a consumer-driven art, public taste provided a natural selection of marketable imagery. But it was the artists' interpretation and expression of those scenes that sold them. The entrepreneurial painters would capitalize on some half-dozen archetypical scenes of Florida that they arrived at through a process of distillation which began at Backus's studio. These views served as templates and were explored under many qualities of light and weather to become the artists' own. As rudimentary forms they encouraged the very act of painting.

A few of his pieces depicted people at work and play at home, bordering on genre painting, but they didn't satisfy buyers at that time, although today some collectors covet them because

of their scarcity. If these pieces had sold well, many more would have been produced. These rustic, often stereotypical, pictures of blacks distanced the viewer from nature, so these representations were the antithesis of the emotional need that landscape art filled. As Harold Newton found his way, his paintings became his calling cards.

Newton's early landscapes often depicted a prehistoric land. His birds appeared like winged reptiles from the Mesozoic era. Sometimes he used a palette of "technicolors," bright pigments applied in short strokes to achieve an Impressionistic effect of light and space and an immediacy of being there. His images entered a viewer's subconsciousness to question whether one had actually ever seen that particular landscape or, perhaps, the image of it somewhere else, as if it resided ancestrally trapped deep within. Daring and experimental qualities mark these works. He then painted with a vigor that was more emotive than representative while being veracious, but without any claim for photographic fidelity.

Such paintings explored the nature of sight, as the experience of light perceived allowed for an awareness of place. But as his palette became more sedate, cool, and detached, the images were without subjective and expressive overtones. Thickly applied paint gave way to smoothly graduated surfaces. These delicate and beautiful images were seemingly accurate and transparent, like looking through a window. These looked like the places people knew, without doubt. Viewers, in fact, enjoyed personalizing the paintings. Some were apt to testify to a painting as representing a specific place, although the paintings were, almost exclusively, archetypal images.

For viewers to identify with the land depicted required that the imagery be palpably real. None were more "real" than Newton's. His relatively exalted views drew into the process the spectator, who in turn was elevated to arbiter. The land became

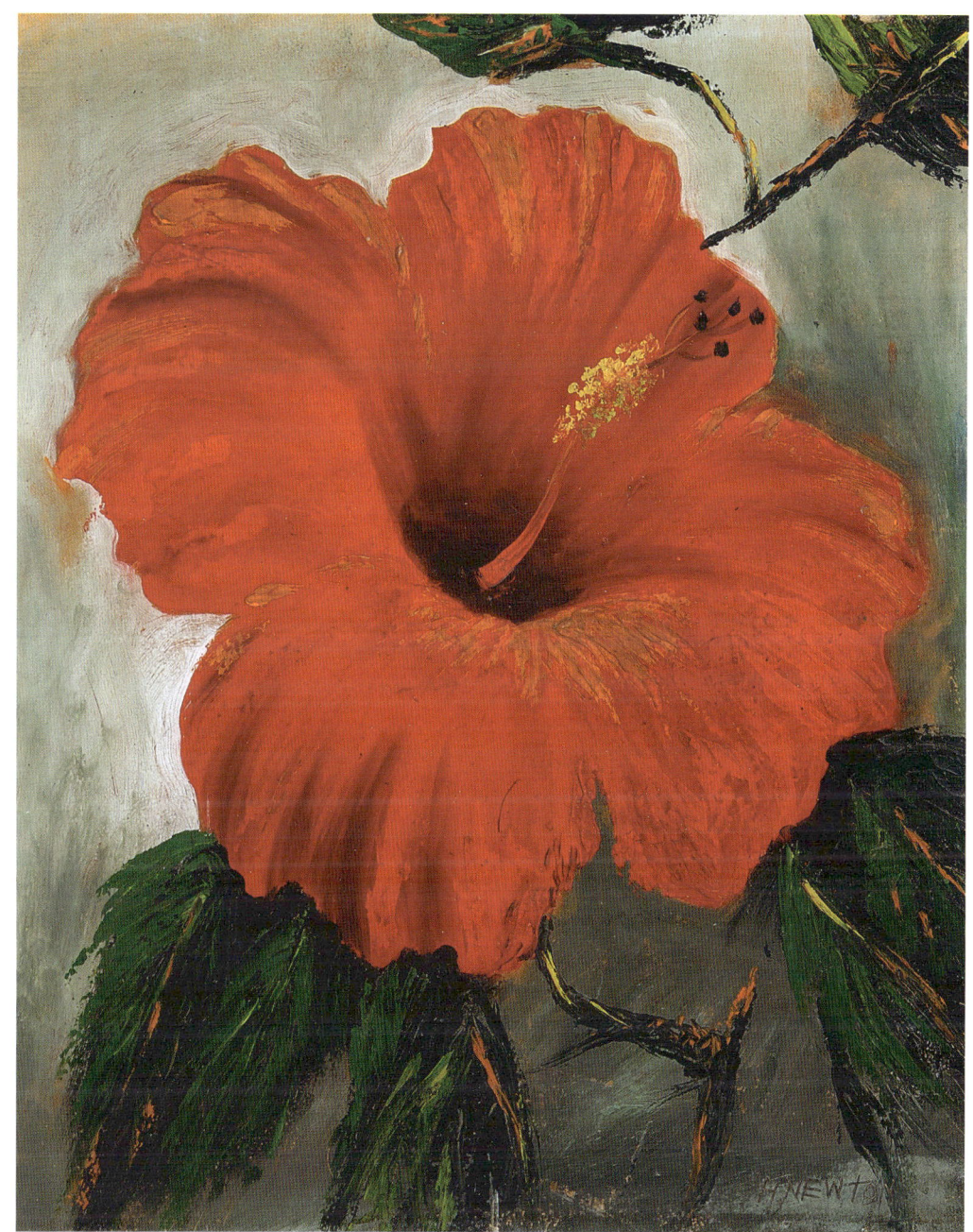

Hibiscuses were one of the few ancillary subjects that Newton had painted. 21¾" × 17¾" oil on Upson board.

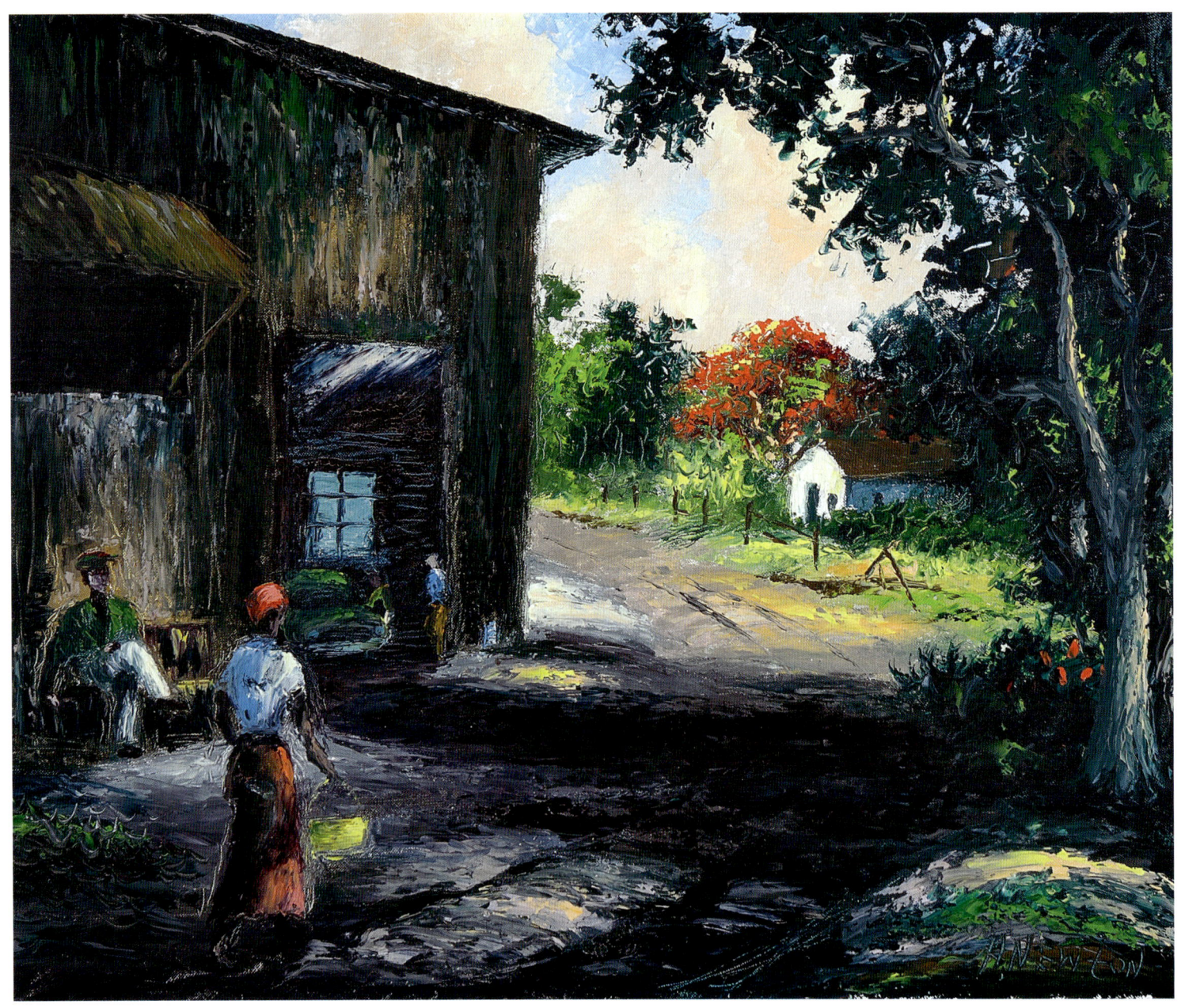

Paintings of daily activities constituted a slight output for Newton. 19⅜″ × 23½″ oil on canvas board.

the domain of the viewer. Lending their own meanings to the images was automatic and wonderful. This ability stimulated the sale of paintings while empowering people to have a say in their own destinies. This emboldened spirit was necessary while people flocked to Florida during the boom years to find a reality often at odds with their dreams and the advertisements that sold them and Florida real estate.

Although he was creating a product for an artistically unsophisticated audience, Newton ultimately painted for himself, and his pictures were his own. With so much practice and, at times, perhaps a lack of motivation, the near-technical perfection that came easily to him resulted in some safe and predictable paintings. This is a reality for any working artist of long standing, especially one so prolific. But his prosaic scenes are the exception. No two paintings are alike. He went on to explore the infinite offerings of light and space available for forty years.

Harold Newton stands alone, having created the images of modern Florida that symbolized the state as the place to really be alive, to raise a family in its fecund wilds, and to find solace as one looks back at life in retirement. Florida was the Promised Land. The artist possessed an unmatched ability to define the state's meaning and natural beauty in iconic dimensions. This is his legacy.

Andrew James Newton was born on October 30, 1934, in Gifford, Florida. He didn't know that his name wasn't Harold until he was in his fifties. Having to appear in court for a minor traffic violation, he waited most of the day for his name to be called. Finally he asked the clerk if he was at the right place on the right day. The clerk told him that there was no Harold Newton on the roster, but there was an Andrew James Newton on the list and he was in contempt. It appears that Harold's father preferred the "less snooty" name of Harold to his mother's choice, the one recorded on his birth certificate.

Harold was one of fifteen children born to Rachel Newton. Rachel's husband, Fred, who was thirty-seven years older than his wife, brought three more children to the marriage. The Newton family moved from Gifford to Tifton, Georgia, his parents' hometown, in 1940, when Harold was seven, because the government had bought the land on which the family was living for a planned but never actualized airport.

Gifford had been settled because, as researcher Pam Cooper points out, "many former slaves left the repressed conditions of the Carolinas and Alabama knowing that for the first time they could own land and be free. These were people who were strong and willing to fight the system of black oppression by owning and living off the land. Gifford was energized and growing with enthusiasm and pride in those early years of 1890–1920s."

Dorothy Collier Newton remembers: "Gifford had a fish house, a theater bigger than the one in Vero, a drugstore where you could sit and get ice cream, a dry cleaners, a lumberyard, a grocery store, a department store, a health department, and a post office. You didn't even have to go to Vero then to pay your electric bill; didn't even have water bills back then." In fact, Vero Beach, a coastal town, was a secondary concern to Gifford, whose high and fertile ground promised a rich future.

Whites came into the community during the 1930s, and race relations began to deteriorate. It was a vibrant community until World War II. Then Gifford did not age like Vero Beach in light of, or because of, the laws that promised equality but supported segregation. When Harold was a youngster, Gifford was composed of orange groves and paths cutting through fields to small wooden homes with well-tended gardens out back. According to Dorothy, "It's a ragged town now."

"Gifford was nothing but bushes and sand. Just dirt roads. Paths. We used to call 'em paths," says Dorothy, as she explains how she met Harold. Their mothers were good friends, and the children regularly played together. Even then, Harold was the artist, drawing pictures of cowboys riding horses on his school papers, often to his teachers' dismay.

His mother recalls, "He loved to draw. When he got tired of studying, he drawed pictures at the end of his lessons. He didn't get in no trouble." She wrote poetry and was a talented seamstress, and she supplied young Harold and his siblings with paper to encourage their artistic development. Harold's first pictures were done with crayons. He was entering "Draw Me" newspaper contests and was winning them with regularity. In the seventh grade he tried his hand at portraiture.

When his father died, Harold dropped out of school and helped support the family. He returned alone to Gifford in 1951. He thought of Florida as his home and a place ripe for his art.

Harold had three passions: painting, fishing, and women. He embarked on all of these upon returning to Gifford. He worked in the groves to support himself. He drew and painted with water-based colors but soon graduated to oils. He found solace and inspiration through fishing, a sign perhaps of his independent spirit, which was about to bloom.

Dorothy remembers reuniting with Harold one Sunday morning while on her way to church. She was in her backyard when she saw someone in the distance sprinting toward her. As he got closer, she excitedly hollered, "I know who you are!" The teenagers started making up for lost time and, she says, "We fell in love all over again." They took long walks, and Harold drew pictures of her. Soon he got down on one knee and proposed. She said yes.

Dorothy had to tell someone, so she told Harold's aunt Nancy. But the aunt discouraged Dorothy's mother from allowing the marriage by telling her that she had "better not let that gal marry that boy; he's going to be just like his daddy," keeping her barefoot, pregnant, and out of college, contrary to what he had promised his bride.

Dorothy says, "We were holding hands and crying." Since his mother seemed open to the marriage, Harold appealed to Dorothy's mom, but to no avail. Aunt Nancy told her, "He'll have her in Georgia plowin' behind mules." They were too young to wed, in her opinion. They went to their pastor. Even his intervention failed. Harold and Dorothy continued their romance: "We didn't give up."

The aunt persuaded her sister, Harold's mother, to call him home to Tifton under the guise of needing him to care for her during a feigned illness. It was a ploy to separate the young couple. Harold and Dorothy wrote to each other; he said he would be coming right back. While there, though, "he asked a girl an unfair question, something he didn't have no right to be asking." She became pregnant with Harold's first child. He told his mother that he still intended to marry Dorothy but that he would also provide for his child. His mother thought differently: "If you mess up a cat, you're going to marry that cat."

Whether it was a willing alliance or a shotgun wedding, he and Caronias White wed. He was seventeen years old. Harold then began painting Christian-themed pictures on velvet. At $2.50 apiece, he wasn't selling enough religious scenes at local churches to support his new family, his mother, and his siblings. He then tried to sell them from the road, thereby setting the Highwaymen's sales precedent. He worked in the tobacco, cotton, and peanut fields as well as at a car lot to make ends meet. According to Marjorie Silver, who wrote the only known feature article about the artist before his death (*Miami Herald*, February 15, 1959), Harold found such work "distasteful."

Harold had painted his first large landscape on a wall of the family house in Tifton, a pond set in a green meadow, flanked by deer at each side and unified by oak and pine trees. He and Caronias rented a small house next door. But one windy day late in 1953, when their front door was left open, the curtains blew into the fireplace and caught fire. Flames destroyed the house. Nineteen-year-old Harold told his mother, "I'm going back to Gifford where I was born."

As Harold's drama began unfolding, Dorothy made plans of her own to reclaim her love, plans that were, in a sense, Shakespearian. She wanted to see Harold more than ever when she learned of his marriage to Caronias. Opportunity knocked in a bizarre way.

"You see, I, too, married someone I didn't love. I married him to get to Georgia," Dorothy says. She wed Harry Collier. Their mothers were friends. In fact, Harry and Harold were friends, too, having worked in the groves together. "Harry went to following me around, to the store, even to church. I got to wondering why." As a crew boss, Harry would follow the crops northward. The Eastern Shore migrant flow began at Homestead, just above the Florida Keys, and extended into New England. So, she said, "he offered to carry me with him next time he go to New Jersey." To avoid "people talking," Dorothy agreed to marry Harry, essentially and admittedly "for a free ride to Georgia," to be near Harold.

Meanwhile, Harold and Caronias, with their baby, Carolyn, were en route to Gifford, like many other families who were moving to Florida. With the postwar boom in full force, people were upbeat about their prospects in the Sunshine State. Harold Newton, primed to capitalize on the population growth and expanding economy, was about to become a professional artist. What followed might aptly be considered a mythic odyssey, at least to those who have fallen in love with this art during the past decade of the Highwaymen resurgence.

Harold paid particular attention to the landscape when he returned to Florida's central east coast, where Amazonian vegetation meshed with moss-draped oaks hanging over river banks. Romantic idealism boosted northerners' confidence as they settled this new frontier. Gleaming under radiant light, the land as painted suggested the primordial wilds, and this inspired newcomers to think of themselves as pioneers.

"I stomped on more than I sold though back there in 1953 it were—before I met Mr. Beanie Backus," he had told the reporter. Upon a visit to Backus's studio, in downtown Fort Pierce early in 1954, influenced by the relative wealth and fame that Backus had acquired with regional imagery, Harold embarked on a career as a landscapist in earnest. Suddenly he stopped painting images of Jesus walking on water.

Backus, whose door was always open to everyone, an action that was especially notable during those times of civil strife, was using a palette knife to spread paint and build images. This was new to Harold. Although Backus didn't offer him instruction or advice, he allowed Harold to watch him work. Harold would soon do the same for the other aspiring black artists in the area.

Harold bought a fruit knife at the hardware store, thinking it a viable substitute for a palette knife. Eventually he got the courage to go to an art supply store and purchase a real one. This must have been a rite of passage. Soon he wielded the artist's knife to achieve results that he found liberating.

It didn't take long for Harold to develop the requisite skill to work with oils. His creative growth was facilitated by further visits to Backus's studio. As Backus had done during the lean war years, Harold painted on inexpensive Upson board, a thick cardboard used for interior construction, instead of on canvas, which he used infrequently. By the late 1970s he was painting on Masonite.

Harold's virtuosity amazed those who were trying to make a go at painting, especially Alfred Hair. But Hair cared less about artistic excellence than about mass-producing paintings to make lots of money. Hair spent leisure time with Newton, the two racing their cars and socializing together, but he also spent time watching Harold paint, as if to learn by osmosis. Newton said that Hair's palm trees looked like they were about to fall over.

Meantime, Dorothy and Harry had come back to Gifford. Harold and Dorothy lived parallel lives, seeing one another less and less often. Neither marriage was good. Dorothy stayed with Harry because they were having children, and eventually she raised five boys and one girl. Caronias, by all accounts, was vitriolic. She was easily set off, even by Harold's lightheartedness. They had three children together: Carolyn and the twins Helen Rose and Harold "Bro," who were born in Gifford in 1954.

Harold left Gifford in the late 1950s to live and work alone in Fort Pierce. He and Caronias lived separate lives. But he would keep in touch with her intermittently, as he would do with other women in his life. "He would come visit. Didn't care if Mom got mad. I know he loved his kids," remembers Helen Rose.

Harold was painting but not doing much selling in the beginning. Business picked up quickly, though. To sell his paintings, Harold called on doctors, lawyers, and other professionals, and sometimes people called him. He would make appointments to go to their homes. He would also go to banks, real estate offices, telephone companies, or any other business where large groups worked so that he could appeal to several potential buyers at one time. He was developing an expanding customer base, and word of mouth was bringing ever-fresh business his way.

When he began his artistic foray, Harold priced his paintings at $10 each; this would later escalate to $75 and more. He would keep his prices a few dollars higher than the emerging artists who were taking his lead but with a more aggressive stance. Perhaps, though, they were keeping their prices down to be competitive. Harold would accept lower prices, especially late in the day. Bartering worked, too. He did so to pay medical bills, including for his babies' births, and as down payments for cars. He seldom went home with any paintings in his possession at the close of a sales session, but when he did, his head would hang.

In the 1950s, Gray Brewer moved to Titusville to work as a court reporter. The Treasure Coast was "all back-country," and his job took him to many regional courthouses. He saw landscape paintings signed "H. Newton" wherever he traveled, often in judges' chambers. Brewer was determined to meet the artist and buy paintings. He drove around Fort Pierce and wherever he heard Harold might be. It took him a month to find the artist.

One Saturday, Brewer stopped by a corner store in Gifford. "I drove up in a Cadillac because it was the best go-cart I could find. There were twenty-four or twenty-five people standing around. Everybody dropped everything but their candy and ice cream. They looked at me and asked, 'What are you doing here, Whitie?' I said I'm looking for Harold Newton. One man asked, 'Anybody know Harold Newton?' Everybody said no. 'I don't know him' was the standard answer." They weren't offering an outsider such information. As he walked away, two youngsters ran up and told him that Harold Newton lived "right dare" and pointed down the street.

Brewer found the artist at home. It was the beginning of a lifelong friendship. He doesn't remember buying any paintings then, if there were even any to buy. "But the next time I did, and the next time, and the next time." Harold soon started coming to the Titusville Courthouse, usually with four paintings to sell. Brewer thinks their friendship opened the northern region for Harold.

It is difficult to tell whether Harold was always on the go primarily to sell paintings for income to care for his children, a number that was steadily increasing, or because he had an insatiable wanderlust. It is likely the latter. Harold gravitated north to sell his paintings while most of the other painters went south. South Florida offered increased marketability given the affluence of the big cities, such as that found in Palm Beach, Fort Lauderdale, and Miami. But Harold had other ideas.

Harold preferred the more laidback north because the roads offered great views and great fishing. He passed through Melbourne and Titusville to Daytona Beach and sleepy Flagler Beach, and inland through DeLand, Orange City, and Sanford. He avoided the pitfalls of competition this way and the web that the carefree younger artists might weave.

It is a worthwhile exercise to examine exactly who are Highwaymen and how each painter falls into the Highwaymen hierarchy. They were young African-Americans from, or associated with, the Fort Pierce/Gifford fraternity of painters from 1960 through the early 1980s who, to varying degrees, embraced Harold Newton's artistry, having taken to the streets to sell their paintings of the surrounding landscape. Since the group's borders were amorphous, some critics view the number of listed Highwaymen as generous, while a few others, mostly area painters, think it slight.

Roy McLendon, James Gibson, and Livingston Roberts were the first to paint with Newton and Hair, making these five artists the original Highwaymen. The others joined as word spread of their undertaking. But without a formal association, which might have had rules or taken dues, identifying where each painter fits into the scheme of things, classification of the Highwaymen is a knotty proposition. The qualifying divide is involvement, and this translates as quality and productivity of paintings and relationship to the cohort. Harold Newton pro-

vided a model that, if not antithetical to Hair's model, was superior to it by traditional standards because Hair's prototype characterized an extreme of Highwaymen marketing and aesthetics. He put Harold's model in warp drive to unintentionally but meaningfully alter it. However, it would be wrong to discount Alfred Hair's role because he gave wings to the disenfranchised blacks who left a unique collective vision of modern Florida. Harold was the first and the finest, traditionally speaking.

Mary Ann Carroll was inspired to become an artist after watching Harold Newton "bring color to life" as he painted a Royal Poinciana tree on Seventeenth Street and Avenue Q in Fort Pierce, where most of the black artists lived and socialized. She came onboard soon after the group formed, but she should be considered a core member because she was the only woman and she added a lot to the collective oeuvre with her color sensibility.

Willie Daniels and Al Black also were central to the action. Although Daniels was relatively young, the quality of his work epitomized the Highwaymen's ideal. This was not surprising, since he lived next-door to Newton and McLendon and often watched them paint. His works could be mistaken for Newton's; his technical skills are superb. Al Black began painting after 1970, having sold aggressively for most of the other painters until then, and thereby kept, if not set, a frenetic pace. He says that he learned to paint by repairing paintings that had gotten smudged while in his possession for sale.

These artists established the Highwaymen style, a look and feel that differed from professional and academic models. They are responsible for originating the distinctive dreamscapes, whereas their peers seemed to emulate them, taking their cues from the raw energies of this core group who took their cue from Harold Newton. Needless to say, the common folk who were the Highwaymen's customer base preferred the tried-

and-true renditions to the sketchier and gutsier interpretations that resulted from fast painting. These artists could complete a painting in minutes, utilizing Hair's modus operandi.

The core painters' imagery shook the foundation of the prosaic landscape model to arrive at a fresh aesthetic, creating a virtual artistic movement. Newton's paintings epitomized the best of conventional imagery because of their certain flair, inextricably and inexplicably altering his depictions with a quality of incantation. As James Gibson points out, "If it wasn't for Harold, we wouldn't really have been painting. He could paint better than we could." He acknowledges, "People were looking for Harold's paintings; they were always preferred."

Harold's brother Lemuel admits, "Sam and I wouldn't know nothing about painting if it weren't for Harold. All the painters wouldn't know nothing about painting if it weren't for Harold, including Alfred Hair." The amazement that the other artists felt about Harold is clear from Mary Ann Carroll's statement that "I never saw a human do that with his hand. Everybody else was a Johnny-come-lately." Besides brandishing standard artists' tools, "Harold painted with a chicken feather—anything he could put in his hand," says Gray Brewer. "I got a spoon he used."

Willie Daniels states, "Harold was number one. Everyone wanted to be like him. Masterpieces off the top of his head." James observes that "you can put Harold's and Mr. Backus's paintings together, and you'd be surprised."

Harold knew that he was good. However, he didn't suffer from hubris. The egotistical aspect of art making didn't affect him, as if being an artist gave him a direct line to God. He didn't sport a black cloak and beret. His standard attire consisted of shorts and a cowboy hat with two short feathers stuck in the band. When he wore long pants, usually blue jeans, he pulled on his cowboy boots. When it came to his art, he didn't want anyone telling him what to do. "I have to please Harold," he would say.

"It was his way or no way," says Sweetie Jordan, his girlfriend during the mid-1960s. He would be annoyed if she offered constructive criticism. She wanted him to open a studio to sell his pictures; she offered to decorate the space. But Harold didn't want that kind of contact with the shopping public. Sweetie even questioned the cost of the paintings, saying, "They look like they're worth more, two to three times as much." But Harold would snap, "Be quiet!" or say nothing.

"He hung to himself a lot. Grouped up when he went to Eddie's," Fort Pierce's once popular juke joint, remembers Willie Daniels. "He didn't have much to say," says Dorothy. "He didn't bother anybody. He was shy." James says, "Newton's personal life I didn't know much about." He picked his friends. Willie says, "Harold didn't work around nobody," meaning other artists. He was closest to Livingston Roberts and Roy McLendon. He encouraged the others but didn't discuss painting, nor did he criticize or offer much advice. "All Harold said to me was lower the horizon," says Willie.

Harold would withdraw from the world by going into the woods, in the community of Oslo, just north of Fort Pierce, where he had a trailer. He would vanish for days to paint in solitude. He was a private person, perhaps a loner at heart. In the evening he might go to Eddie's Place or into Gifford to have a beer and relax at The Green Leaf.

On Friday and Saturday nights, Eddie's was a lively hangout. On Avenue D, young black men and women would arrive in style and either slide into the benches, where four people could sit on each side of a table, or walk up to the bar, where Eddie Asbury would be serving drinks, a cigar hanging out of his mouth. Whenever Harold said or did something funny, Eddie would shift the cigar from one side of his mouth to the other, like when Harold would break into the Cooter Hop, a dance he invented. Some patrons would shoot pool, others would dance to the music from the jukebox, and many would cavort inside the large smoke-filled building until late at night when they spilled out into the parking lot.

"Loved his Cadillacs. He had a brand-new brown Eldorado. Harold was the only black man in Fort Pierce who had a new Cadillac. He parked it right up in front of Eddie's and bought everybody beer," remembers David Lundy. "The boss-man's in," Harold would announce. Lundy recalls Harold "lining the counter at the bar full of beer," and telling the denizens, "By the time you drink that I'll be back." Lundy goes on: "Harold would go outside and paint a picture real fast, sell the picture, and come back—just that quick—and spend it." Harold would regularly walk into the bar and say, "Eddie, set everybody up and put it on me."

Harold attracted a variety of people. Sweetie relates, "People would gang around and look at him paint whenever he tacked up a board. A number of them learned by looking over his shoulder—Mary Ann, Alfred, Livingston, and Sam. I thought they were trying to get something from him." It was as if he possessed arcane secrets that only he could offer. Sweetie would ask, "How do you do that?" and Harold would reply, "Just watch me."

Others, not just his fellow artists, revered Harold. For example, when there was an art show at a shopping mall, people often recognized him and exclaimed, "My God, that's Harold Newton," even though he had no paintings on display. "Like they'd never wash their hands again. He was the talk of the town," at least to the people who bought paintings from him and lived under their spell.

"I paints when I'm hungry—but then, I'm always going towards hungry," Harold once said. When he needed money, all he had to do was get on the road with some undoubtedly still-wet paintings. Once, while on the road, a policeman pulled Harold over for speeding. The judge found him guilty and bought two paintings on the spot so that Harold could pay the fine and get back on the road. He crossed Florida like a sailor off to exotic ports of call.

Harold enjoyed driving around in his big cars. He would arrive at a sales destination and show his paintings to professionals and laborers, who would readily buy them. Willie offers: "He didn't have to work old customers. He could make new ones." Realtors bought paintings as housewarming gifts to present at closings to new homeowners. Admirers would swear that Harold Newton's paintings changed hues throughout the day, as if iridescent.

As some of the painters honed their skills, after working an eight-hour day of a forty-hour week, others drifted away from painting. At the same time, Harold was building a following. Sweetie says that "the rest of them made a lot of paintings, just put together," as opposed to Harold's pristine interpretations. "Looks like you could just jump into his," she says of one painting, describing the inimitable way that the "warm glow is set off by the pine trees, how the sunlight hits the trees."

In the 1960s and 1970s, these artists' paintings appeared exponentially throughout the region and beyond. Back then, all such landscapes were generically called Newtons. It has been said that some of the other artists, besides his brothers, called themselves Newton.

Sweetie states, "Harold was a person who liked to roam around and explore. When he got tired of one place, he'd move on. He'd stay in one place a pretty good while. Then he'd move on. From Gifford to Fort Pierce, to Melbourne, then Daytona Beach and to DeLand, where we engaged but never married. He followed me!" Harold liked his women around him. Harold liked them near and far. He could not have opened a gallery, as Sweetie had wanted, because he couldn't be tied to one place.

There were two Harold Newtons—the artist and the socializer. These two really didn't mix. He was quiet, even withdrawn, when he wasn't drinking, and very serious while painting. But with alcohol consumption he became a livewire. His youngest sibling, Bonnie Brothers, points out that although Harold was the life of the party, he may not have been truly happy, and that is why he would go off and start another life, time and again. Her husband, Dale, adds that Harold had relationships and children "all up and down the coast." This, having been said, was not to impugn his character, which their daughter Brenda describes as "down to earth." She says, "Every time he would see us, he would give us money. He was real sweet." Dale adds, "Give you the shirt off his back, a humble person. Harold would reach out to you." This assessment is incontrovertible.

Harold's friend Willie Monds concurs: "He was just a real nice person. He liked to keep everybody laughing. He kept everybody interested, never offended anybody." He told jokes. One of his favorites was a story he told with conviction.

One day I was driving down the road in the country and there were three people, and I hit all three. One landed in the cow pasture. One was down the road. And one was in the windshield. I was feeling sad and upset when the police came. But the policeman said, "Don't worry now. I'm going to ticket that one in the field for leaving the scene, the one down the road for trespassing, and this one here in your car for breaking-and-entering."

In spite of his outgoingness, Harold didn't talk very much. Beer would limber him up. Dorothy points out that he would be transformed with a few swallows, "He would talk, talk, talk." He was funny with a beer or two in him. He didn't regularly indulge in liquor, so it was easy to tell if he had drunk one too many. He might take two hops to the side and say, "Who pushed me?" Harold would tell jokes in the juke joints. He would call a buddy over and say, "Last time I saw someone who looked like you, his mouth had a hook in it."

Harold Newton loved fishing. Dorothy reports, "He'd catch fish where no one else would. He could go right up and pull 'em in." Dorothy, who enjoyed fishing with him, says that "he wouldn't catch but three: 'One for me and two for you,' he'd say." Sweetie enjoyed reading a novel when she accompanied Harold, but he didn't like that. He wanted her to watch him catch fish. Sweetie couldn't understand Harold all the time. "He would get up at 4 a.m. and go with his fishing pole. I think he was looking for scenery." His brother Lemuel agrees that the quiet waters inspired Harold. "The creeks and lakes, that's where he got his ideas from."

Harold would go fishing if he wanted peace and quiet. He would remark that "the early bird catches the worm," and off he would go. When he worked, Sweetie says, "He'd be singing, singing, singing, painting, painting, painting. His mind was on nothing but painting. He'd chew tobacco, whistle, sing. No liquor." He was "always sober when he worked," says niece Shirley Jackson. "Not a drop when painting. He didn't touch it while working, including selling," says Dorothy.

Willie Monds affirms that Harold loved to fish and was very good at bringing them in: "I knew he was a better fisherman than I was because he caught more fish." They would drink together during the late 1960s at the Silver Dollar, a bar in Cocoa. "Oh, now he was a good friend. That Schlitz beer. I couldn't drink with him. I couldn't keep up with him." Gray Brewer says that when Harold sold a painting, he and his friends would go to the bar and stay there until the money was gone. Brewer remembers Harold's brother Sam saying, "Harold didn't have any friends. He just had drinking buddies."

There may be something to Sam's wry remark. David Lundy remembers Harold, though, as a man who "just loved to help people." It was a time when blacks, especially in agricultural Fort Pierce, toiled but still had no money. Lundy relates, "We'd catch the bus to Belle Glade to do field work." Harold, on the other hand, was jovial as he pulled out wads of cash, "rolls of $100 bills," and announced, "'You all come in and have a seat, gather around the bar.' We would drink three or four hours without spending a dime." Harold would even walk around and give everyone there money. "He'd put two or three dollars in your pocket." It was a generous gift then.

Dale Brothers recalls a group of men sitting beneath a big shade tree one summer and Harold telling stories as they relaxed with cases of beer. In one story, he said he was pulled over by a policeman because of a broken taillight. He said he accepted the ticket and informed the officer, "As soon as I get that taillight fixed, I'm going to get me a license." Then, he added, "My wife cut in and told the policeman 'Don't pay him no attention 'cause he's drunk.'"

Dale observes, "I knew he was a good painter from the Cadillac he drove." He adds, "When he painted he was totally serious. No drinking. No joking. He was totally focused inward. A different person." Sweetie concurs, explaining that if someone said something that distracted him while he was painting, it was only momentary. He would glance at him or her but turn right back to the board, undeterred, as if no one was really there.

Mary Ann Carroll says that Harold and a few of the other Highwaymen, including Livingston Roberts and George Buck-

ner, "didn't just paint for the buck." This is echoed by Gray Brewer's observation that "Harold painted and thought differently about painting than the other artists. The others were in it for the money. He painted for himself, at his own pace, when he felt like it." Harold was disciplined and concerned with the quality of his art, teasingly expressing his pride to his closest friends. Sweetie says, "He named himself the Greatest Artist in the South." He could also claim to be among the most prolific.

The number of paintings that Harold Newton made is indeterminable. Family members and fellow artists, including James Gibson and Harold's niece Shirley, saw Harold paint "three, four, or five pictures a day." The consensus is that Harold painted in spurts. Dale saw Harold "turn out a lot of paintings. Two or three days doing that. Depending on how badly he needed money he'd go out on the road and come back with a pocket full of money, a stack of money." He adds, "When cash goes, he might paint a few right quick."

Harold painted a picture for his friend Gray Brewer. As Harold tacked an 18"-by-24" board to the side of the house, Brewer glanced at his pocket watch. It was "right on the hour." Harold made a final brush stroke sixty minutes later, moss hanging off an oak tree limb. He walked back a few steps and said, "Guess that'll do it. You work too much, and it'll mess it up." The image was of a lone pine stand in front of which a pond surrounded by grasses and a scrub palmetto balance off an impasto sky that swirls with a hint of Van Gogh.

Although Harold Newton could have at least made substantial progress toward realizing Alfred Hair's dream of working feverishly to become a millionaire while young enough to enjoy such wealth, he preferred to get by and enjoy living in the moment. He would paint a big picture or some small ones in the morning, then go fishing. Harold would load a few paintings in his car to sell, and then he would likely call it a day after they had been sold, no matter how early it was. By contrast, the other painters would only be warming up at this time, not stopping until each of their stacks of paintings was sold.

"He painted every week, maybe not every day," Mary Ann says. James believes that Harold tended to paint three days consecutively. It was typical for some of the Highwaymen to do so to amass a framed crop of glistening oils to take on the road on Fridays because that was payday. Dorothy recalls, "Harold painted about every day, when he wasn't selling." It was his job. He depended on painting for his living.

Sweetie recalls Harold painting "two or three at a time in four to five hours. He could turn them out fast. He painted every day for a few weeks, in painting bouts." When Harold painted in the woods, he would be certain to have enough room to be able to step back from a work in progress, assess it, add to it, or make changes. This required as much as ten feet. He would wear a path in the thickets as he painted and painted, walking to and from the board. "Every time he touched a board, he had to back up to see what it looked like," affirms Mary Ann.

Sweetie adds, "He'd start in a corner, and you don't know what it'll be. He'd keep backing up, looking sideways at his paintings, all the time chewing tobacco, whistling, singing." Harold would jest, warning her: "Get out of my way when I get ready to spit my tobacco out!"

Of course, the paintings looked better framed. Harold and the others would construct their own versions of frames from the inexpensive trim that carpenters use for finishing doors, windows, and floors. The molding was usually whitewashed and then streaked with gold paint to "antique" them. Not only did the frames improve the looks of the paintings but they also allowed the paintings to be stacked, thereby safeguarding them during transport, when they would be tossed around in the backs of cars. Since the images were painted on standard sized boards, the paintings of similar dimensions nested, one in the next. The frames prevented scratches, smudges, and other damage while in transit.

Harold didn't especially like making frames. Because he enjoyed going to yard sales and thrift stores, he sometimes bought used frames. Therefore, his paintings didn't necessarily sport Highwaymen-style frames. Sometimes he would embellish these secondhand frames by rubbing pigment into them so that the frame would enhance the painting. Still, those he crafted were sturdier than those made by the others, including people whom the artists had paid to make their frames. The one exception was a "notched" frame constructed by their friend Lincoln Allen. He made one-inch notches running along the frames' edges.

Even Harold's signature had flair. Positioning his left hand beneath his right for support, both suspended above the wet paint, he was free to incise his signature—first initial followed by surname. This was the rule among the cohort, and it was done with rusty nails or other kinds of styluses. For reasons unknown, Harold didn't cross his t's after first penning the vertical stem of the letter. Rather, he started with the horizontal part of the letter, followed by incising the stem.

Harold liked to work during the cool of morning. He tended to paint at home, tacking a board onto a tree or tacking one or two boards onto the side of the house, if not painting on the porch. Harold might return to certain spots he had seen during afternoon drives to see how these places looked in the morning. The scenes were transformed. The light was radiant, its modeling effect most pronounced with long and dramatic shadows, when the sun was nearer to the horizon.

The Highwaymen's strength as colorists resulted from their not having learned color theory; hence they were not restrained in their use of colors. Their slapdash approach didn't give them the time to be overly concerned with mixing pigments to perfection. Harold Newton, however, did blend his paints with deliberation. Furthermore, his observational powers were exceptional.

Gray Brewer once asked Harold why he put orange in the palmetto shrubs. Newton replied, "That's the way they be." Indeed, at sundown the plant might catch the light to reveal the warm glow and, as Brewer points out, there is an orange tint at certain times of the maturity of the plants. "When you got to looking, 'that's the way it be,'" he adds. To those who criticize Harold's palette as being extravagant or inaccurate, the ninety-eight-year-old Brewer exclaims, "They are not." Some detractors may never have witnessed a Florida sunset and those few seconds of unearthly colors.

Lemuel says, "Harold painted by moods. Harold painted when he felt like painting." Sometimes he didn't want to paint. Sometimes he would cook, instead. Sweetie says, "He would eat live oysters and make a grunt while swallowing each one. And he'd cut an onion in rings, dip them in vinegar, and chew 'em up. He didn't cry." He would bring home blowfish that he had caught, season with salt and pepper, and bake them until very brown, when the inedible fish would look delicious. Then he would show it off and go to the back door and throw it as far as he could, getting a kick from his own antics. Harold's favorite meal, remembers Shirley, was boiled pigs' feet. Dorothy says that he used plenty of vinegar in everything he cooked.

Other than fishing, Harold did not have a lot of leisure time pursuits. He didn't care much for television, but he loved Saturday morning cartoons. "He was worse than the kids. He wanted to see if Coyote would ever catch Roadrunner," remembers Sweetie. He also had stacks of comic books.

But if reading the adventures of Superman, for instance, kept him awake at night, he would awaken Sweetie with "Young'un, let's go out." He would go to a bar and get a miniature bottle of vodka or gin. Reports vary and tend to exaggerate Harold's consumption of alcohol. Usually he was a social drinker, but he would drink to excess when he was with his sister Annette.

Harold lived in his own right-brained world, eccentrically and with a sense of humor. Sweetie reports that Harold would blurt out: "I'm so good, sometimes it scares me!" Such "Eureka" moments were jovial, not expressions of arrogance. "Harold never thought he was better than anybody," says Mary Ann.

Moodiness could be understood as "an artistic temperament," but the term is nearly meaningless if not dismissive. Perhaps aloof or elusive are more accurate descriptions. Harold's so-called moods may have been mistaken for the idiosyncrasies of an impassioned person, although he may have suffered from mild depression and thereby had personality shifts. Dorothy admits to his ups and downs, but she says that Harold wasn't moody: "He talked too much to be moody. He was never moody with nobody. He had people laughing all the time. At parties people would be listening and laughing at his jokes." Of course, at social gatherings he would have had a few drinks.

When he had imbibed a little too much, he would tease Sweetie by elbowing her and asking, "Where's the ashtray," knowing very well where it was. He was just playing, perhaps being affectionate. She would tell him, "There it is, right next to you." When she had had enough teasing and he had gotten under her skin, she might tell him to take his beer and get out. "But he'd be right back. It was his way to annoy me."

Sweetie points out that "sometimes Harold was hard to get along with." He had his moments like anyone else. He didn't want to be bothered at times, like when he was engrossed in painting. And he could be edgy. For example, he might respond to a compliment on his new car with "What's it to you?" instead of a simple thank-you. But then he would turn around and offer the unfortunate recipient of the remark a cold beer. Harold's quips were generally a good-natured way of joking, attracting attention, like when he would tell a buddy, "When I leave, I want you to lay down so I can have something to walk on." Or he might instruct a friend to "call me Mr. Newton." Harold was always enjoying himself. Sweetie wonders "if somebody spoiled him before I met him."

Harold never found himself in the doghouse, at least not for long. "He'd romance you. He could act so nice. Like he's tiptoeing on soft-boiled eggs," says Sweetie. He could endear himself. He would turn a bottle upside-down and squeeze it, pretending to get the last drop out. He was a joker. Dorothy says, "He'd tell me nice jokes. When he'd be with his friends, he'd tell bad jokes." It seemed that Harold's women were upstanding ladies. In fact, Mary Ann said that she liked most of them: "They were all nice, except Caronias."

In contrast to observations made by Harold's friends, Caronias's co-workers describe her fondly. Helen Rose explains that her mother was a pleasant person who "took a lot from my daddy," indicating that her mother's angst and temper resulted from Harold's philandering: "There was a bunch of women. That's why he and my mom didn't get along."

Harold identified with Sam Cooke's soulful music and would often be singing verses from the great recording artist's most popular songs. "Another Saturday Night" could have been his anthem. "Good Times" mirrors his artistry and philosophy and perhaps his penchant for wine and women. He saved "Jesus Be a Fence around Me" for painting.

Harold went on the road selling without his artist-friends. He might take a girlfriend along. "We'd go out selling. He'd lean them against the car," Sweetie remembers. "The housewife and husband would say, 'They're so gorgeous.'" She says that Harold

often fidgeted while showing his paintings. He didn't seem to know what to do with his hands when he wasn't holding a brush or catching fish.

Harold Newton became a staple in many communities and in many people's lives. "He was well known—whites and blacks—by his paintings," says Willie Monds. Those were times of growing racial tension, a time when up the road in Mims, civil rights pioneer Harry T. Moore was killed on Christmas night in 1951 by a bomb placed beneath the bedroom floorboards. His wife, Harriette, died the next week. The sparks from that bomb ignited a call for equality before Martin Luther King's charismatic speeches, Emmett Till's whistling at a white woman, and Rosa Parks's refusal to move to the back of the bus.

Harold wasn't stigmatized by race as he traversed the state selling his paintings during those charged and uncertain times. Gray Brewer explains, "Harold wasn't a black man. He was a painter who happened to have dark-colored skin. And he knew how to get along with everybody."

He left behind original Florida art, art about Florida for people who did not have art in their daily lives, along with warm personal feelings in a hostile environment. The unsolved bombing case that took the lives of the Moores was reopened forty years later, just before Newton's career abruptly ended. He lived and worked under the daunting specter of racial inferiority, but he prevailed with grace. Had he lived a decade longer, Harold would have driven past a billboard on I-95 calling for tips about the murders that were of another era, a time and mentality he helped to change.

The Highwaymen's story transcends race. It is about art and commerce—paint, pride, and profit. It is punctuated by colorful characters who charted untraveled territory. None were more colorful than Harold. "So many people knew him. I just mention his name, and they'll give me a story," says his sister Brenda.

In the early 1960s, Paul Raible, a general contractor in Vero Beach, built a home for Dr. Blumenthal, a retired dentist from the north. Dr. Blumenthal was so pleased with the house that he wanted to give the contractor a gift. When asked what he would like, Mr. Raible replied that he would like a painting just like the one hanging in Dr. Blumenthal's home. The doctor quickly educated the younger man when he said, "Paul, artists don't copy. They create." Nevertheless, Dr. Blumenthal was happy to acquire a painting for his contractor.

Both men went to where Harold Newton was working. Raible saw a painting with a royal Poinciana tree, but it had no people and no clothesline in it like the one hanging in the doctor's home. Harold immediately added those features to a painting for Raible. For many years, Raible entertained his children with the "artists don't copy, they create" mantra.

Raible's painting now hangs in his son's living room. It shows an African-American woman hanging laundry to dry on a clothesline that stretches from the wooden house to a post in the near foreground. A little boy in diapers chases a ball. A dirt road trails off into the woods, behind a royal Poinciana tree. In the left midground are two shanties, in front of which is a man. All are under a typically beautiful Florida sky, with shadows cast as long as the figures are tall.

Many stories abound regarding ownership of Harold Newton's paintings:

- A man sees his neighbor's lawn being mowed and asks to have his yard mowed, too. After doing so three times, the man who mows lawns for a living finds the man whose grass he's been mowing at home and asks to be paid. The man says

he's short on cash but offers three paintings in lieu of money. He walks away with three Harold Newtons—from the artist himself.

- A couple buy a house and, upon moving into the empty place, notice something shoved behind the water heater in the garage—two Harold Newton paintings, which they return to the living room.

- A couple divorce, and the man is awarded only three of the twelve paintings that he, a dentist, bought from Harold to decorate his new offices. He says, "Now I have one in my bedroom. I look at a sunset every night as I turn off the light."

- A vice president of a central Florida bank retires. For a going-away present, he requests a painting that has been hanging in an office there for years. The board is unaware of the nature of the largesse, so he walks away with a stunning Harold Newton painting under his arm, complete with a grazing steer anchoring the heartland.

These incidents probably would not occur today, because fewer and fewer people remain unaware of the Highwaymen and Harold Newton especially.

Another professional, John Bennett, asked Harold to come to his office in Rivera Beach. "Each time he would offer me first choice of three to five paintings and I would always buy one. My memory is that I eventually had eleven or twelve paintings. Currently [in 2004] I have six. My ex-wife had two or three and gave one away. I sold one in 1966 and another one recently [to an art dealer]. My largest and best one was purchased at his mother's home at Gifford, Florida. I never saw Hal again."

Many people gave their Highwaymen paintings away or threw them out. Some buyers expressed more interest in the frame than in the painting.

In 1996 Diana Flagg stopped at a Holly Hill garage sale only because a "hideous painting of a ship" caught her eye, and she needed a frame. The frame was plastic, but nearby lay a wood frame that was approximately the size she needed. "I didn't know what I had or care who did the work. I bought a frame with an obscured picture covered in layers of dust and dirt. It was marked five dollars, but I offered three dollars, and I wasn't surprised when she accepted it." When she got home, she cleaned encrusted dirt off the painting with soap and water. It was then in excellent condition and "special." But it didn't mean much to her until later when a co-worker told her about the recently brought-to-light group of artists.

She describes the painting: "It looks to me like it is late in the day and the sun is dying out. There are white birds along the shoreline of the river; one is at the water's edge, the other is flying low. In the right forefront there is a palm tree with fronds all brown and lowered to the water. It is signed H. Newton. It reminds me of many places I've been in Florida but mostly of the Tomoka River," which is close to where she bought the painting. "The colors are muted greens and blues but for a splash of late day sun yellow across the sky. I've seen others of these paintings in more vivid colors, but I prefer this one. It brings a thought to me of quiet and calm. I imagine I've sat near that place before." Now it hangs in her office so she can see it often. Someone told her it is worth thousands of dollars.

In 1999, Paul Olson of Flagler Beach retrieved a painting that was in someone's trash. It looked like the nearby intercoastal waterway to him; he especially liked the way the sun's rays illuminated the scene. He took it home, not knowing what he had other than a nice Florida painting. A few years later he saw a painting at a friend's house with a similar frame and asked about it. He learned that he has good taste and that he owned a Harold Newton painting.

Before 2000, folks could regularly pick up Highwaymen paintings at thrift stores and garage sales for as little as a dollar or two. Harold Owen found his in Fort Pierce in 1987. Driving past a garage sale, he spotted a large painting standing on end under a tree. The image appealed to him even at a distance as he craned his neck to see it fully. It seemed somehow familiar, which he attributes to his then cursory awareness of Bean Backus. Just then it began to rain, so Owen rolled down the window and called to the woman holding the sale, asking the price of the painting. She sold it to him for five dollars.

It is interesting how ascribed value changes one's attention to and perception of things. While the Highwaymen were coming into their own, people could conceivably find a Tiffany lamp at a garage sale beside worn children's clothes, tarnished kitchen utensils, frayed books, and scratched records. Art Nouveau was no longer in vogue. Ornate decorative objects were in contrast to Florida's outdoor jalousie-windowed lifestyle, where homes were linear and had open floor plans that were topped with flat roofs. Appreciation often comes late.

Mary Hill first met Harold Newton in the mid-1970s when she was an assistant to the president of Flagship First National Bank in Ormond Beach. Harold would appear unannounced, the guard would notify her, and she would alert several department heads who were interested in his paintings. She says, "He was very quiet, and if you asked him a question, he would answer in few words. I have no idea how many he sold at the bank; however, he kept coming back, so I feel he did pretty well. Then all of a sudden, after several years, we saw no more of him. Harold was about 5'7" with, I'm sure, a lot of Native American blood in him. Very quiet but with black, black eyes that said nothing. There was no way you could get him into a conversation, but I liked him. I often wondered what happened to him. He was a nice man."

Harold told Mary Hill that most of his work was from the St. Johns River, the beautiful American Heritage waterway nearby. It is possible, of course, that the image is of that river. And it is possible that it is not, or it may be a partially realistic rendering of a particular site. Perhaps the artist simply agreed with the viewer, who had projected her own belief into the painting.

Harold may well have been influenced by the river and therefore assimilated its qualities into his pictures. His work, like those by the other Highwaymen, was not site specific, not painted on location like plein-air painters do. Then again, given his astute observational powers, or at least the light that distinguished the scene that caught his attention, it might be based on a certain bend in the river. Many people would swear to it.

Hill remembers, "Every painting would have at least part of a dark sky." She points out that the last time she saw Harold, his blackened skies had given way to unobstructed sunshine. This effect "was more professional" to her, but she found it less satisfying. Her assessment of Harold's lineage is correct. His mother had Native American blood, and his father was mulatto. And, according to the last driver's license issued to him on November 8, 1988, Harold was 5'6".

Doris Conant was sitting under a hair dryer in a Cocoa Beach beauty parlor during the late 1960s when "a small thin black gentleman with a dapper mustache entered." He approached her with several paintings under his arm, asking if she might like to purchase one. She did. "I really fell in love with those paintings. They were so Florida and so natural. She handed Harold Newton twenty-five dollars, all the cash she had in her purse sans the cost of her treatment.

When shopping for "the perfect painting" to complement the new furnishings in their retirement home in Fort Pierce, Ann Bryant wanted one with a Florida feel. In the beachside town of Indialantic, at Frame It, hung some fifteen Harold Newton paintings that were for sale. "They just took your breath away," she says. She chose a seascape instead of one of the gloomy approaching storm scenes; these she found too disturbing. "When sitting and gazing at it, you might think you were just looking out your window at a sunrise over the beach."

She paid $150 for the painting (in 1988) and the same amount to have it framed. The shop owner informed her that Harold was expected to be completing a painting at Frame It soon and that she might want to come for the painting while the artist worked. The proprietor indicated that "she could never be quite sure when Harold would show up." Harold was indeed in the back room painting when Bryant and her husband arrived. "He had just 'Hello' to say to us and went about his painting. He made no response to me when I complimented him on his use of color and tried to engage him in conversation. I'm quite sure he was relieved when we left."

Bill and Monica Rich taped this note to their daughter on the back of their painting:

Holly, Dad had seen Harold Newton's work at an art shop on Clematis St. called the Art Mart. When he returned from Germany he wanted to own one, but Harold had moved. They thought he was in Oslo, Fla. On one of our first dates (Nov. 1963) we drove up [from West Palm Beach] and found the remains of the Oslo Packing Plant and eventually tracked him down to a trailer in the woods. I bought several pictures, and so did Dad. Dad had mentioned that he wanted a storm scene. I asked Harold to paint one that I could give Dad for Christmas. Harold missed the Christmas deadline, so I went up the day after Christmas. The painting with the two pine trees that looks like the north end of the lake used to look like it was nailed to a palm tree. It still had wet paint on it. He pulled out the nail and back I headed to the frame shop. When we were buying all these pictures, we had no idea they would [mostly] all end up together in one house. Dad also has one by A. Hair.

Charles Harris, who managed a national finance company branch in West Palm Beach in the late 1950s, recalls:

We made the mistake of financing a new '59 Ford Sedan (white) for a Harold Newton. I don't remember Mr. Newton ever making a payment on time. Our collectors could never find him. Every time we got a tip on his location, he had moved. We learned that he was traveling about the state in our Ford, selling his paintings. Whenever he could, he would stop for a few hours and set up his paintings. The next day he would be on the other side of the state. You could tell where he had been because you would see his work in offices, restaurants, banks, etc. It was said that he had a girlfriend in every town in South Florida and liked to party (there went our payments).

Finally we caught up with him in Saint Petersburg. He was showing his paintings at a bank. I told the collector to get the money or the car, no promises. We got the car—and what a mess it was. Filthy dirty and he had painted it. The front of the car had flames, but the best parts were the beach scenes. Below the window line he had a beach, ocean, palm trees, and black nude girls running along the beach. This theme was carried from front fenders, down the sides, and across the trunk. The dashboard had also been embellished in a similar manner. The '59 Ford Sedan was a long car, and I am sure he wanted white to paint on. The painting was really pretty good. The car was pretty beat up, and the many dents and dings had damaged the art work. We ended up having the car completely repainted." Who knows what that car would fetch today. Perhaps it would be worth more by the part than complete: $3,000 for a door, $4,000 for the trunk lid, $6,000 for the hood, and the dashboard priceless!

Sweetie's daughter, Sherry Lumpkins, an aspiring artist, remembers her father telling her, "Nobody's as good as Pretty Papa." Harold would remind Sweetie, "I know what I'm talking about. I'm a genius, don't you know." Looking for reassurance, he would say to her, "You don't ever tell me what you think of my work." Her customary reply: "You say you're the genius, right?" Harold would burst out laughing and add, "I am the master."

The master couldn't sit still. He needed his mobility. He lived as far away as the west coast town of Bradenton. Harold had to be productive to help with expenses for a mounting number of offspring, regardless of his need to create art and to experience travel. He tried to maintain close relations with his children, giving them paintings and visiting them as often as he could. He was a loving and concerned father. "A wonderful man, a beautiful person, and very kind," remembers his niece Shirley. He would bring a pocketful of silver coins, throw them all in the air, and let the kids scramble and keep all they could retrieve.

Harold had girlfriends, and many bore him children. Dorothy thinks he had at least eleven children out of wedlock.

Relatives were many, and everyone knew everybody in their small east coast community, so it was easy to keep tabs on each other. Even though Dorothy was married with six children, Harold never forgot her. He visited her when he was in town. She recalls an evening soon after Harold came back to Gifford, also married and with children. While she was having dinner in a restaurant with her husband, Harry, she discovered Harold standing over her. No one said a word, and Harold then walked away like an apparition, vanishing into the night.

Dorothy remembers Harold "walking up to me and saying, 'I am going to marry you yet.'" All she as a religious woman could do was look at him and smile. Years sometimes separated them. But Harold would sporadically reappear. "I would hear someone's car motor real loud. I go to the door and that would be him, and he would look back at me and he would be gone. Next time he come, I hear that motor, I go to the door, that would be him again." One day he came to stay.

Dorothy filed a year before she divorced Harry in 1981. She filed soon after Harold and Caronias had divorced. This was precipitated, Dorothy points out, not by Harold's being unwed but by the murder of her youngest son, who was gunned down at age sixteen. Upon his death, she moved into her sister's home "for a while, to find peace." Although intending to stay there only through the funeral, Dorothy remained separated from her husband. There was no reason to return. Nor did she think about getting together with Harold. "Not at my age—courtin', marrying. My mind wasn't even on Harold."

Having learned that Dorothy and Harry had separated, Harold went to see her in Gifford. "And you know, he kept coming. Carrying me out to eat. Going to church with me. He wanted me to come watch him paint. Sometimes he carried me with him to people's homes" to sell paintings.

Finally, on December 6, 1983, the couple married at the Vero Beach County Courthouse. Dorothy says Harold cried on the courthouse steps. Then and there, according to Harold's sister Rosetta Newton Humphries, he transferred the wedding band that he had worn since marrying Caronias to his right hand.

Dorothy remembers a different scenario: "I bought him a wedding band. He bought me a band, a whole set—engagement ring and band." Remembering Caronias and Harold, Dorothy adds, "He didn't have no wedding band on his finger, and she didn't have one on hers. Maybe he wore other kinds of rings. He didn't have one until I gave him one." Sweetie offers still another version: A tearful Harold would visit her, exclaiming that he had gotten drunk and "woke up with a ring on my finger."

The newlyweds looked for a house in Gifford, but Harold resisted, telling his bride, "I was born here and I don't want to die here." Dorothy thinks he wanted to settle elsewhere because there was "too much family" in Gifford. He wanted to keep space between his wife and sister. Harold and Annette would be "smokin' and drinkin,'" and this bothered her.

They rented a house in Melbourne, and a year later they moved to neighboring Palm Bay. By being adjacent to Port Malabar, a growing General Development planned community, the move proved a good one for sales and solitude. Harold wanted Dorothy to quit her job at the First Baptist Church in Vero Beach, where she had performed domestic work for twenty-four years. She, however, wanted to continue working because work had become a way of life for her. Harold wanted her to be with him, whether at home or on the road.

She would acquiesce within two years, but not because of Harold's insistence. Dorothy had formed blood clots in her leg and was ordered by her doctor to quit working. All the while Harold was the loving husband. "He was a gentleman. He would go to church with me, early on." He hardly drank or smoked at home. Harold told her, "I had to get you some kind of way." He would have breakfast ready for his "sleeping beauty." When Dorothy finally retired, Harold began taking her fishing. He did all the cooking, which he enjoyed. Dorothy wasn't accustomed to the attention that this new lifestyle availed.

I wasn't used to all that cookin' and opening doors for me. Just treated you so nice. I didn't have to buy groceries.

I didn't have to pay bills. Harold told me he was "the man of the house." We was on the go all the time.

We'd go on the west coast. So many places. And up north to sell his work. And when selling, we would get a motel room and go out to eat. Had good times. Sometimes he would have appointments to go to lawyers' homes, doctors' offices, stores, and other places.

People would come to our house. Harold, every time, would go in the kitchen and cook. When they leave, they'd be full. And Harold didn't drink when he is home unless someone came there and want something to drink. He would smoke every now and then, and he would not smoke in the house. But when he goes to other people's houses, he would drink and smoke.

When people came to the house, Harold would stop whatever he was doing, even painting. He would stop everything and prepare a meal. "It could be our worst enemy, and he'd feed 'em," Dorothy says. She amends: "Not that I know of—no enemies." Willie Monds echoes the sentiment: "He didn't have no enemies. If he could do you a favor, he would do you a favor. He was a nice person. He would do anything for you, if he can."

By this time Florida had changed, styles and people's tastes had changed, and the remaining Highwaymen's sales slacked off—except for Harold Newton's. The original artists kept at it: painting was what they knew. But their lifestyles were no longer as fast and furious or as expensive. The core artists, who had painted and sold the most, had the least to show for it monetarily. They had played harder, too. Highwaymen elder Roy McLendon, to this day, paints in the mornings and goes to the Jai-Alai fronton in the afternoons as he, Alfred Hair, and Livingston Roberts had done regularly forty years ago.

James Gibson says, "They couldn't paint with money in their pockets." This seemed to be the case. James was the notable exception—and possibly Harold's brother Sam, who proudly says, "Harold never put down his brush." As artists vanished like they were never there, Harold continued on his journey. However, that would come to a sad and abrupt end.

Harold had high blood pressure and experienced dizzy spells, but he refused pleas from family and friends to see a doctor. One day, he showed Dorothy his forearm: "He had big veins; they look like they were full of blood. But they was not like that no more." Then he began talking in a tone of premonition: "He began telling all the things he was going to do for me—going to church, start working hard. And he was going to buy me a big home, buy me a Cadillac. It was so much he was going to do."

After eating breakfast in a restaurant the next morning, Harold took Dorothy to her hairdresser and continued on to Fort Pierce to sell paintings. He talked incessantly all the way to Gifford, where he let her off. When he picked her up at the salon, hours later, Harold "had a sad look on his face, and his skin looked bright red." Normally he would come inside to banter with the ladies there. This time he was quiet, even solemn. Harold paid Dorothy's bill and they walked outside. He kept looking down, a peculiar look on his face. The couple stood, looking at each other, not saying much, not knowing that this would be the last time they would talk to one another. She remembers him being remorseful, saying "he was sorry how he mistreated other women."

A year apart in age, siblings Harold and Annette had remained remarkably close since childhood. In fact, Harold regularly spent weekends in her Gifford home. It was centrally located and therefore a good place to "crash" after selling paintings with vigor on Friday afternoons when people had cash in their pockets. It was easier than driving home, another hour north, to Palm Bay. And it was a good place to celebrate after being on the road, selling. Dorothy, who didn't drink, would often stay at her relative's house nearby in Gifford.

On the night of February 6, 1993, Harold was at Annette's house when he suffered a massive stroke. Annette called Dorothy to tell her that Harold was being taken to the hospital.

Harold fell into a coma. Dorothy told him, "You can't talk but you can pray in your heart. Pray to God to forgive you for all your sins. Do you hear me?" He blinked his eyes. Dorothy stayed in another bed in the room. She watched visitors come and go. Sweetie remembers Harold's "eyelashes fluttering" at the sound of her voice. With minimal communication—with his eyes, a moan, or maybe an attempted squeeze—he remained bedridden.

Sometimes the physicians and nurses had to revive Harold. As his wife, resuscitation was Dorothy's decision. He must have overheard one such discussion, although the nurse had asked her in the hallway. Something "struck me in the heart." She turned around and saw Harold trying to talk. "He wanted to live." She assured him, "Ain't nothing going to happen to you. I let him know he was going to be all right." Harold was soon sent away for rehabilitation.

Dorothy didn't possess the fortitude to care for Harold in the condition he was in, so she agreed to let Annette help. She remembers a domineering Annette saying, "You trying to take my brother away from me?" She wouldn't put Harold in a nursing home. So, when he left rehab, he went to live at Annette's house. She "would clean his feeding tube that was in his throat twice a day, once before she went to work and then again when she got home," writes Rosetta Humphries.

His daughter Helen Rose went fishing "to the fishing creek, a favorite spot." She recalls that "a big strange bird just stood there and watched me fish. It would not move." The phone rang when she returned home. It was her aunt Sandra calling to tell her that Harold had passed away. Helen Rose remembers that the sky was beautiful that day, like one of her father's paintings. She never saw that bird again.

Harold died at Annette's home at age fifty-nine on June 27, 1994, sixteen months after the stroke. He passed away six months after being brought there, just after "5:00 in the evening when Annette returned from work, as if waiting to say goodbye," Mrs. Humphries suggests.

Without insurance, the man who "lived in the present" died penniless. Annette took out a loan to pay for the expenses. Friends and family and many of his girlfriends and their children attended his funeral. So many people were paying their respects that they couldn't shut the funeral home door. Some mourners came as strangers but left as family. It was an odd family reunion, where younger members met their aunts, uncles, and cousins for the first time—relatives they didn't know they had. Many mourners contributed money to help cover Harold's medical and burial costs.

The African-American Gifford Cemetery is a nondescript space in a nondescript place. From the road it looks like a vacant lot. It has no impressive signage claiming any sacredness. It is unkempt throughout, especially in the back area where Harold Newton was laid to rest. It feels, in fact, like a paupers' cemetery. Filthy white crypts at ground level show wear from being traipsed over and ridden over by lawnmowers, without regard. Many of the plastic black markers, not much bigger than a dollar bill, with their simple dirty-white letters identifying who is buried below and their dates of birth and death, are chipped and falling off, scattered around the weeds like detritus. There are no family plots here. Buried head to toe and side by side, barely a foot separates one from the next, and there is hardly room for a headstone. Only a few makeshift ones stand; some are fallen. All of the dead are laid in order of their demise, like cereal boxes stacked on shelves in the supermarket. A visitor has a better chance of locating a loved one by knowing the date of death than the departed's name.

To me, the blandness of these identical graves suggests that these people never fully existed or mattered. Ironically, as much as Harold Newton did matter, as much as his art is the ultimate symbol for life in the Sunshine State, he was essentially anonymous. And anonymity was necessary for his art. He was, artfully speaking, a medium through which the meaning of the land he described flowed. Although his experiences and innate painterly skill were the core of this art, neither could attract attention to these facts. To achieve this—the illusionism of art—required that his hand not be revealed. The artist's presence must remain subordinate to the image; he could not reflect his own sensibilities or feelings, at least not overtly, through his art lest he show his hand and reveal the illusion. The image and the viewer had to come to one another, as if there were no intermediary, so that the viewer thought that he or she authored the image, perhaps in collaboration with God.

Whatever paintings remain today are testimony to a man who understood, through acute observation of the land, what Florida means, and who possessed the uncanny ability to manifest its essence on board, its coming to life with each intuitive swipe of his palette knife and pass of his brush. It is no wonder that his art garnered attention when it was new and renewed interest today as the images he painted stir emotions about the same places that are being paved over, a paradise lost. Then Harold Newton lived somewhat underground, here and there, a vagabond artist who was developing devotees, all so quietly. His accomplishments were not celebrated. He lived and worked without fanfare. His art led the way to identifying modern Florida, only to be cast aside quietly, waiting for this new day.

The Plates

1. 23⅝" × 29⅝" oil on stretched canvas.

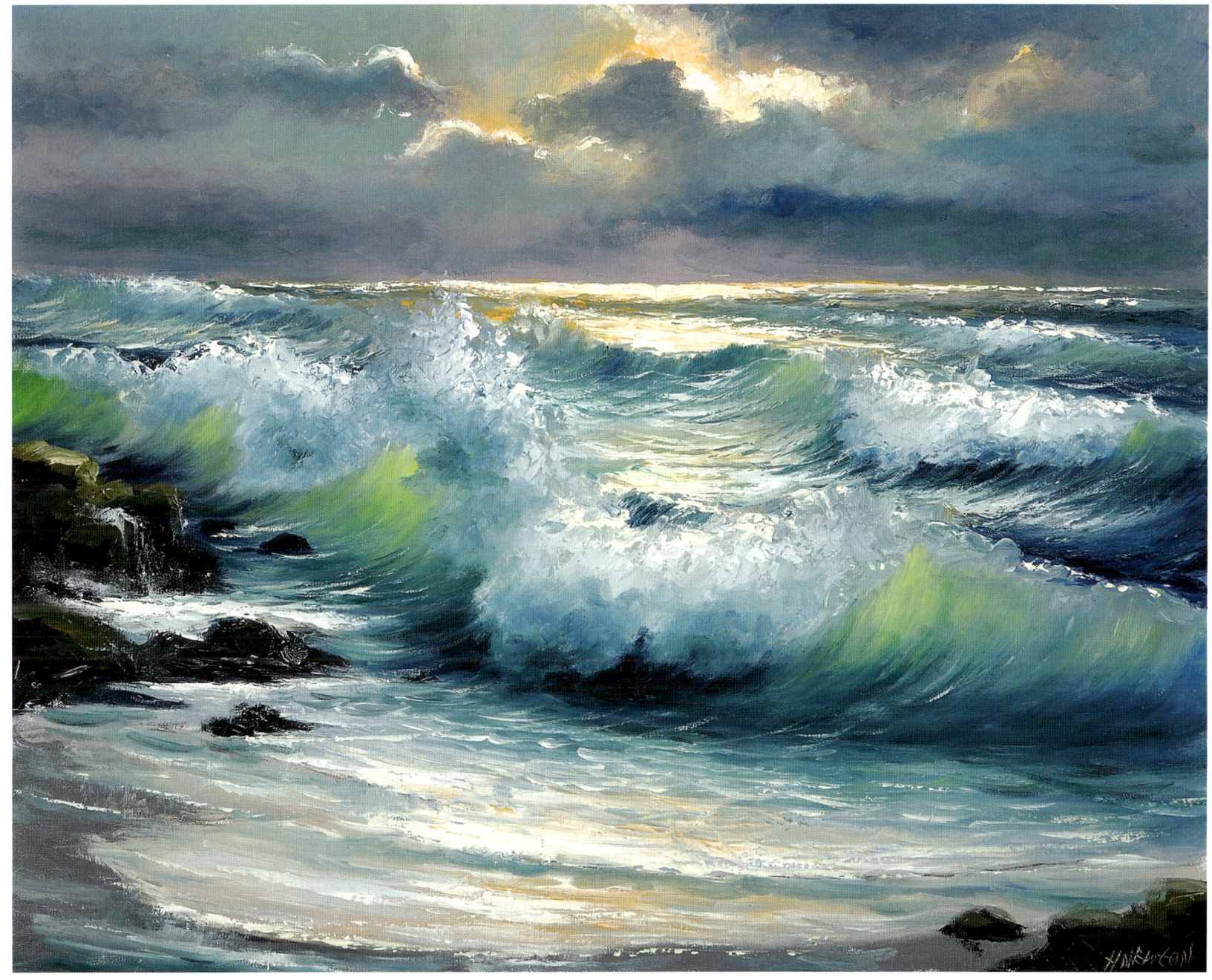

2. 23½" × 35½" oil on Masonite.

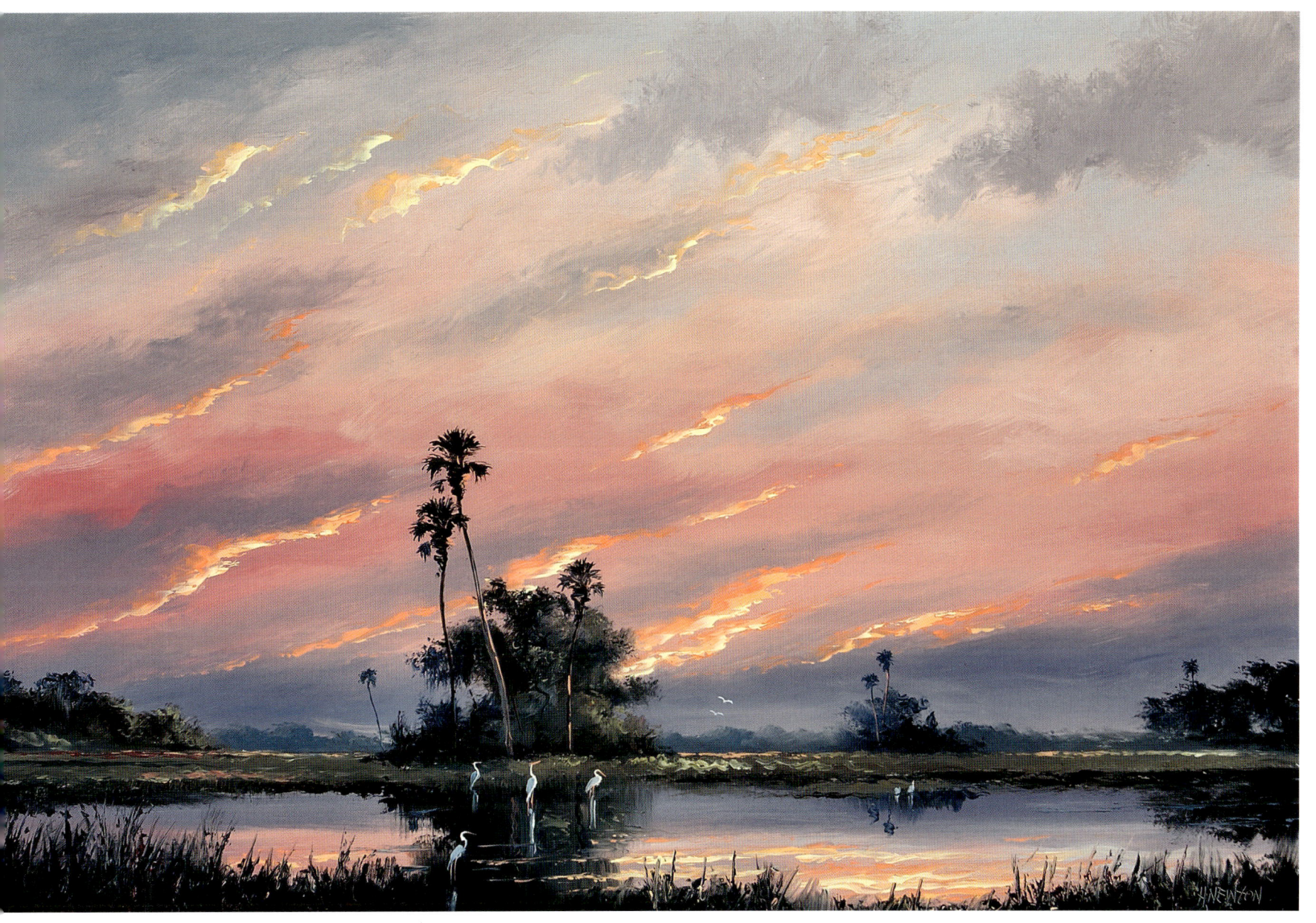

3. 24¼" × 48¾" oil on Masonite.

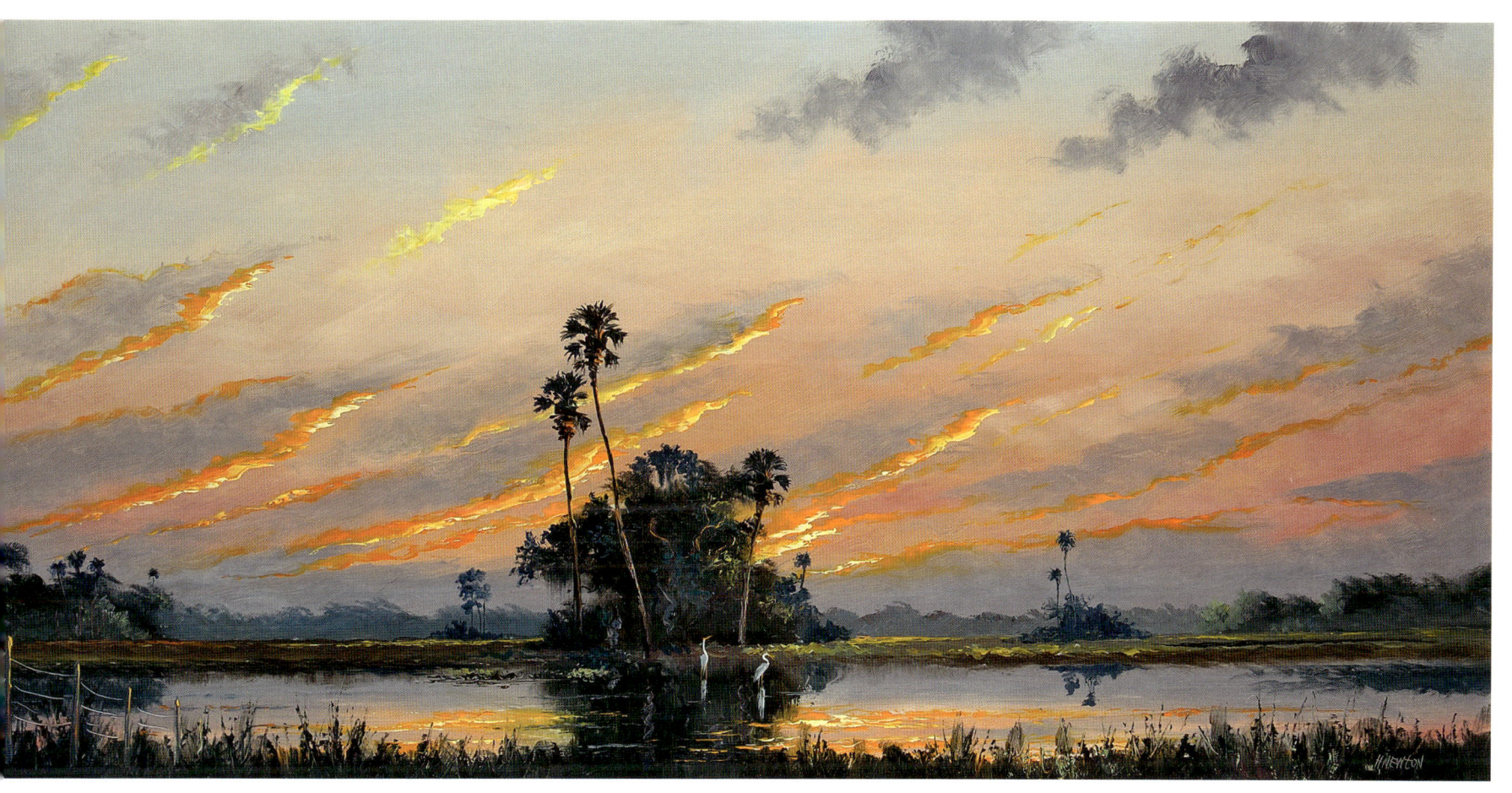

4. 23⅝" × 35⅝" oil on Masonite.

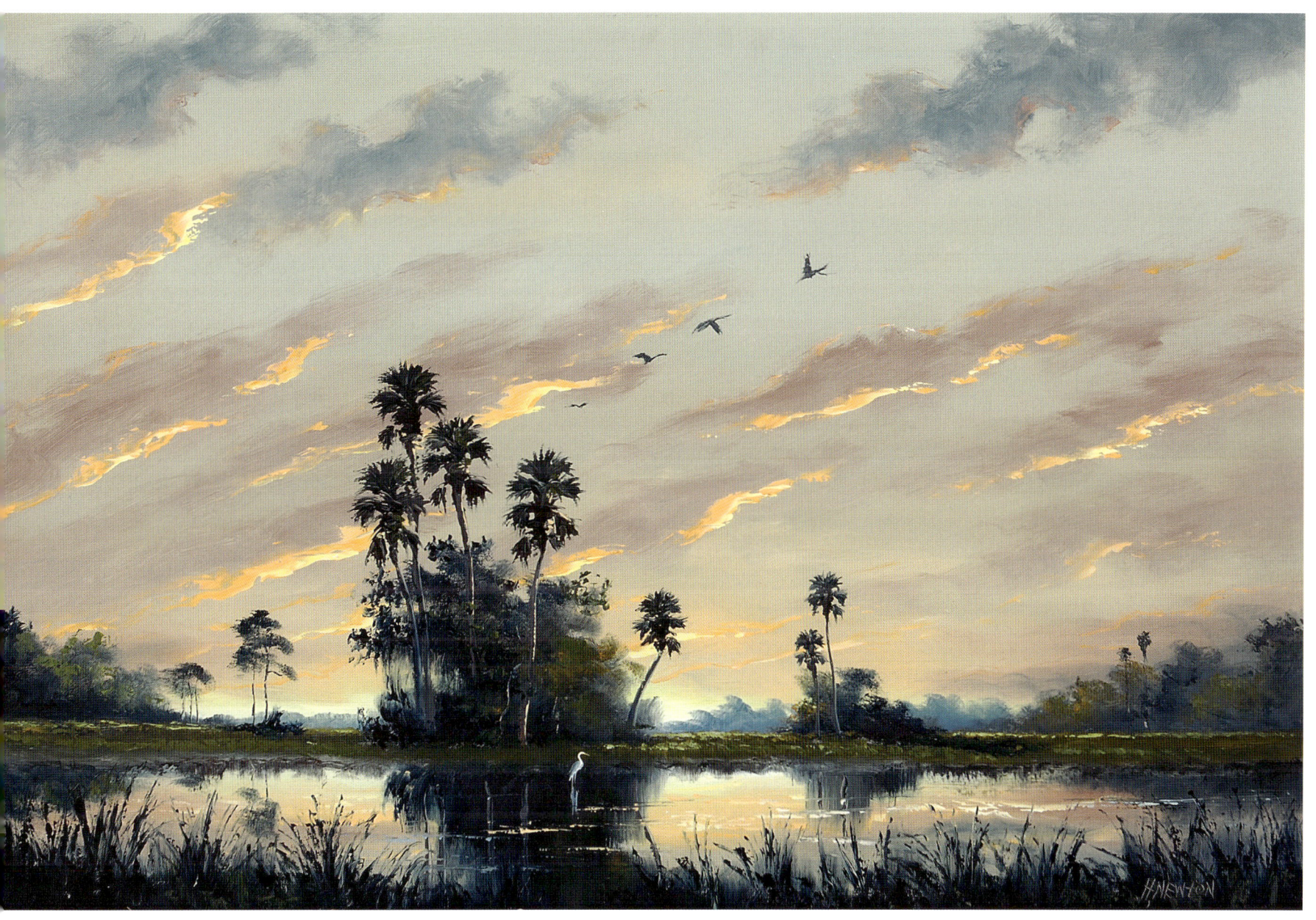

5. 13½" × 33½" oil on Masonite.

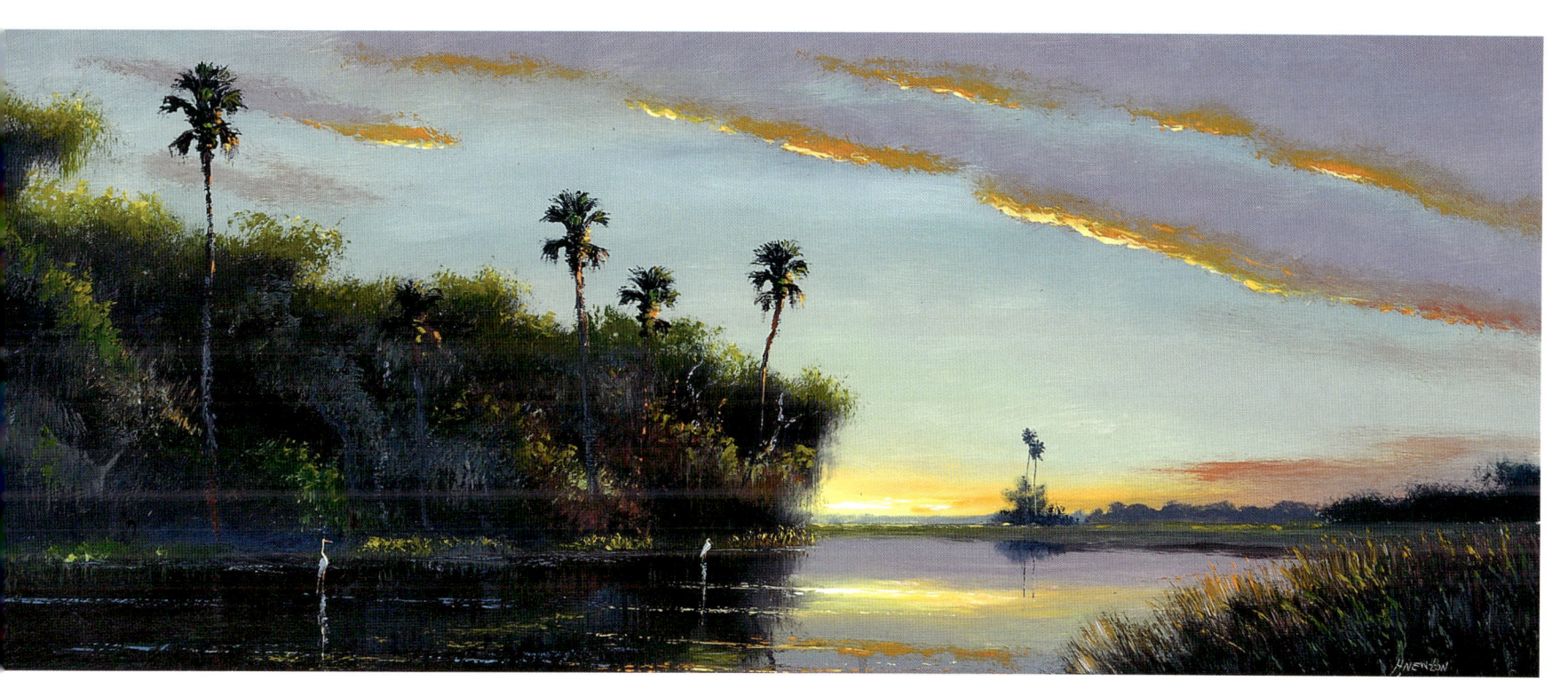

6. 18½" × 14" oil on Masonite.

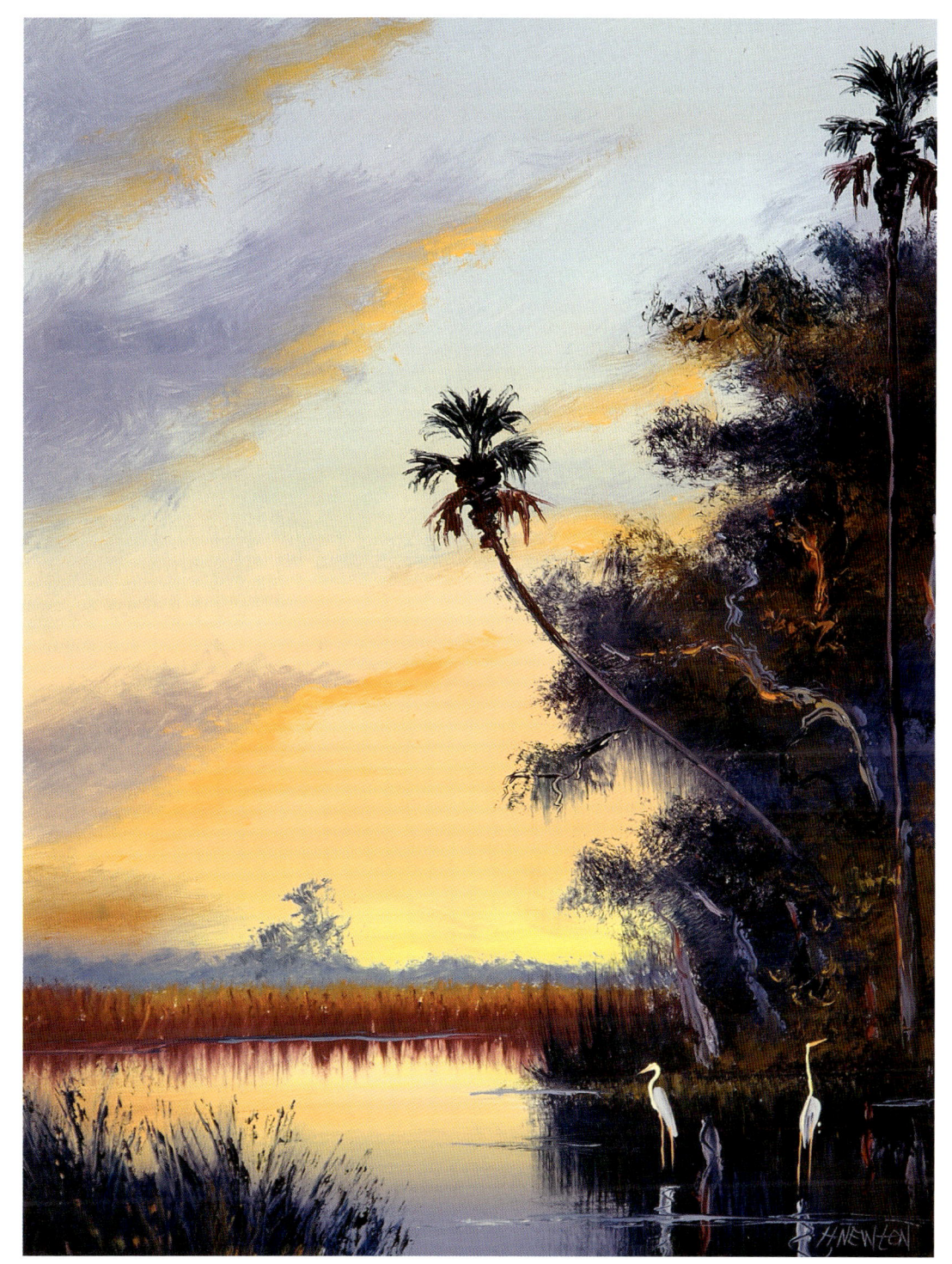

7. 23½" × 35⅜" oil on Upson board.

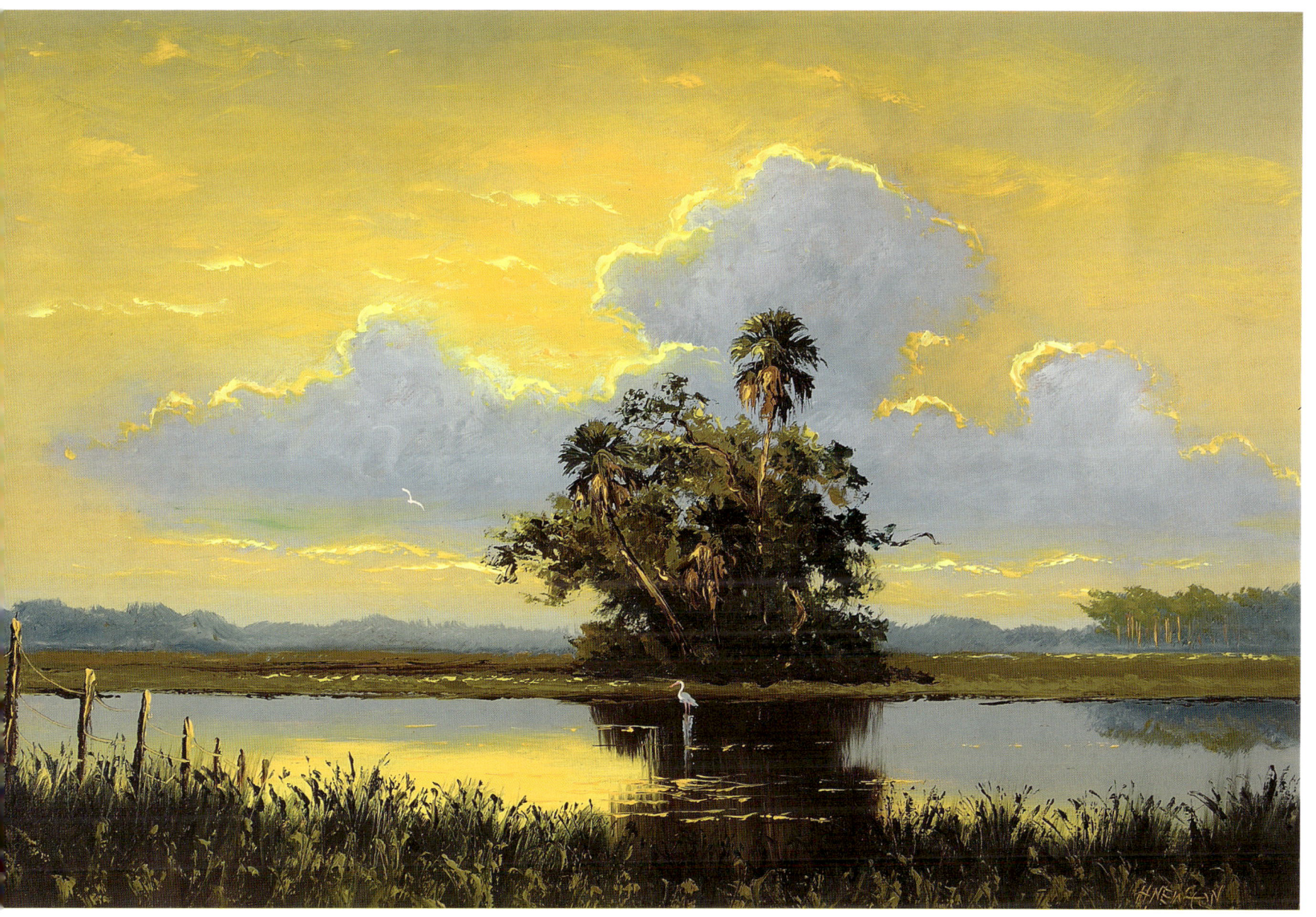

8. 17⅜" × 23⅞" oil on Masonite.

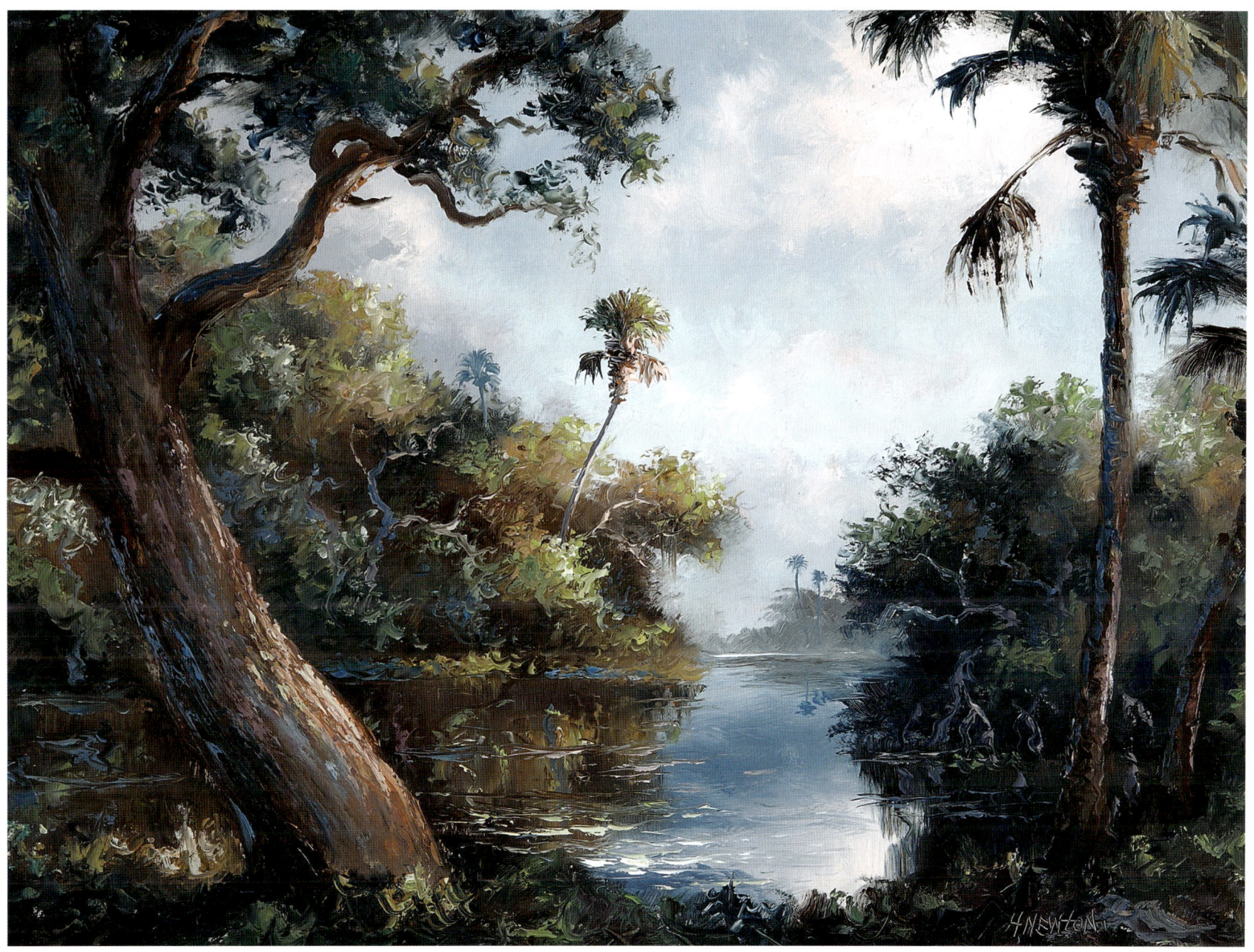

9. 26⅝″ × 35⅜″ oil on Masonite.

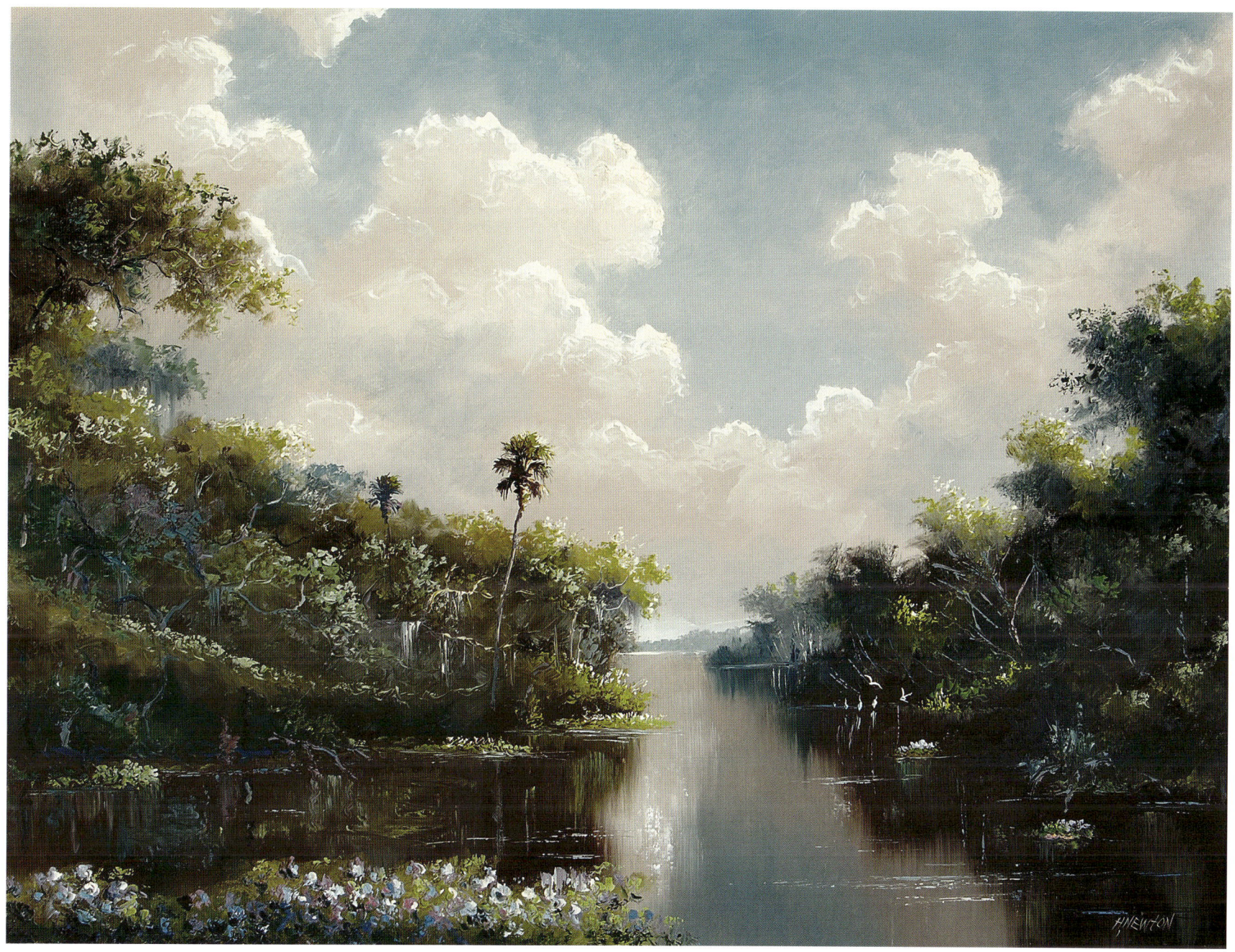

10. 22¾" × 34¾" oil on Masonite.

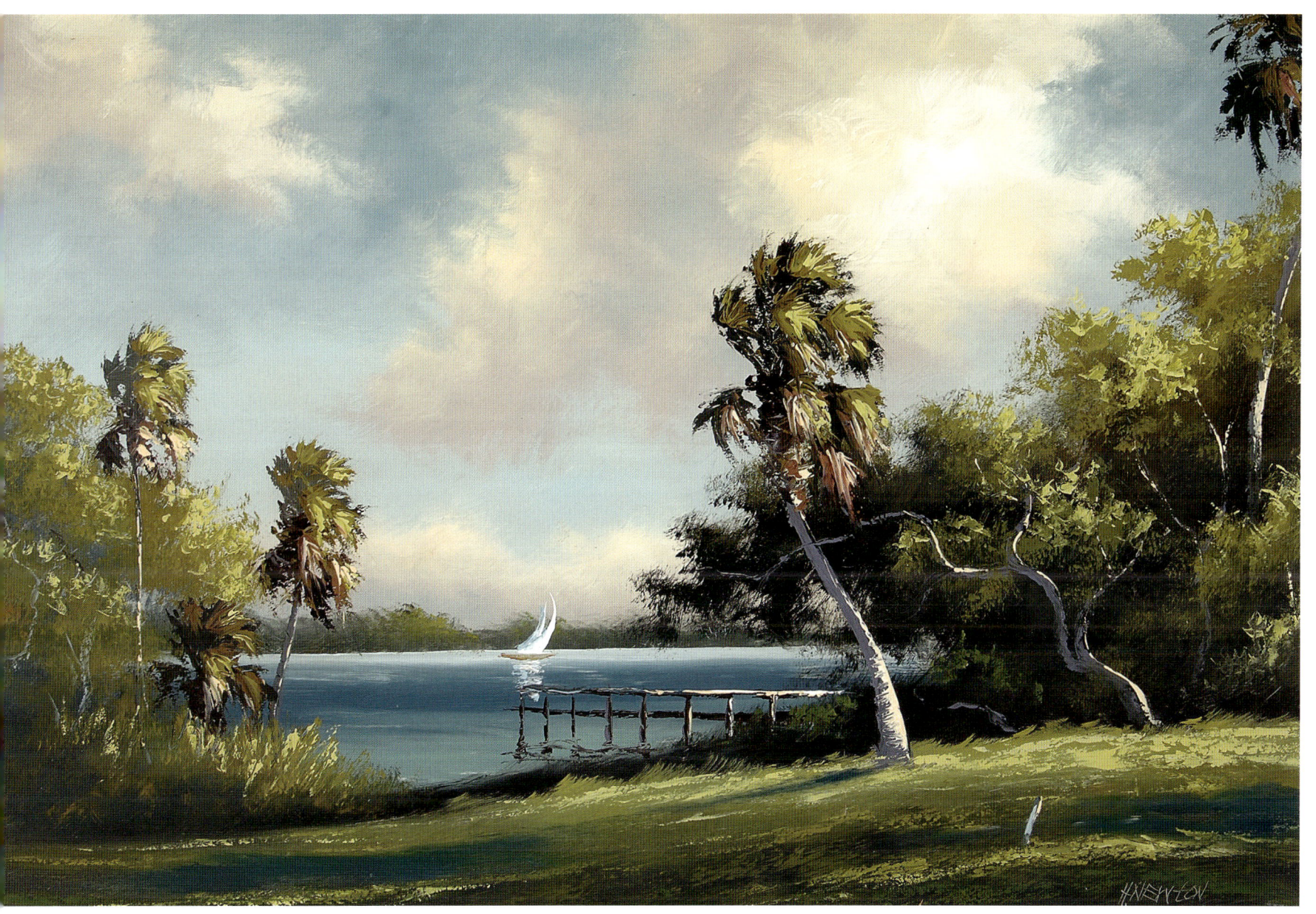

11. 23⅜" × 19¼" oil on Masonite.

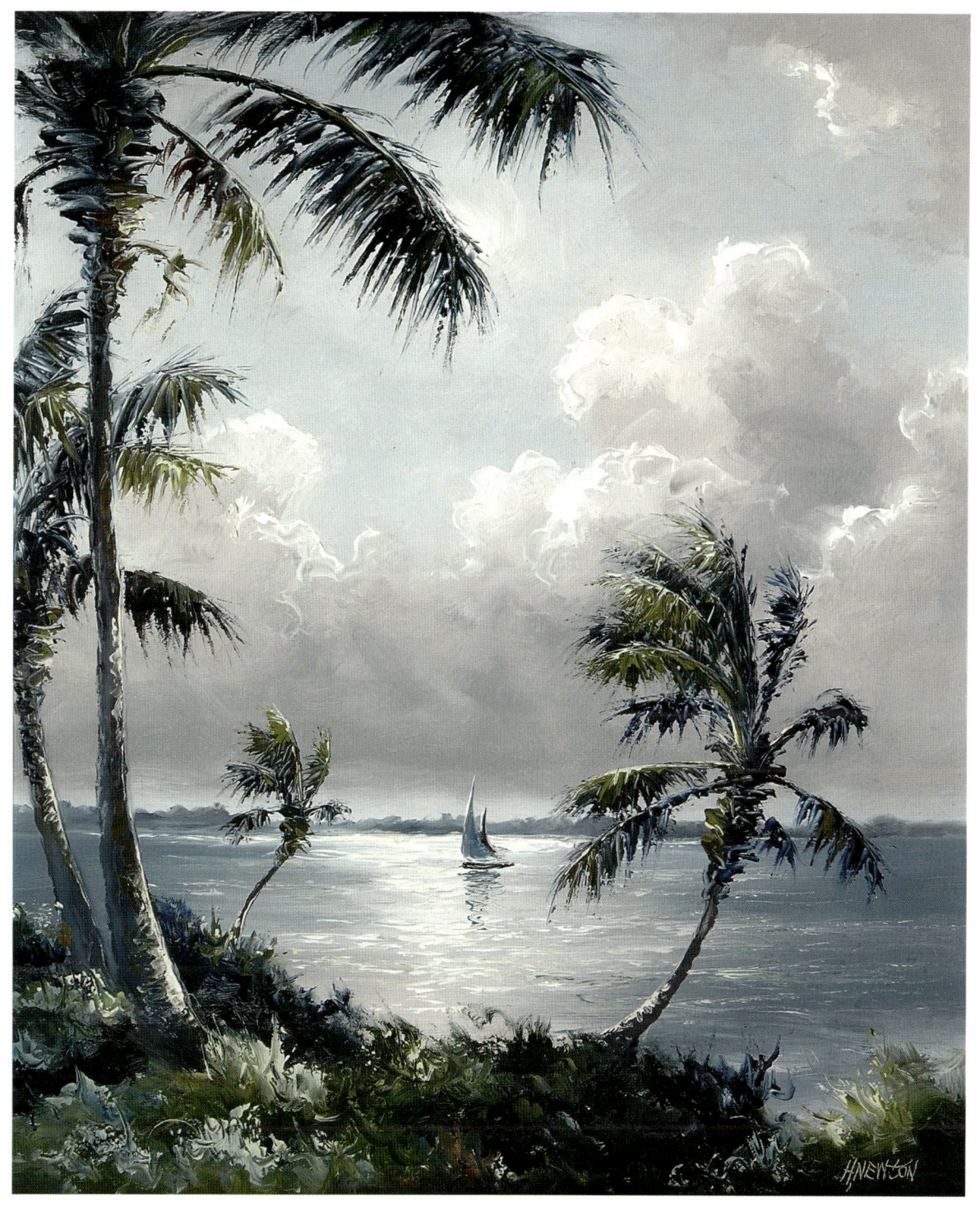

12. 28" × 36" oil on Masonite.

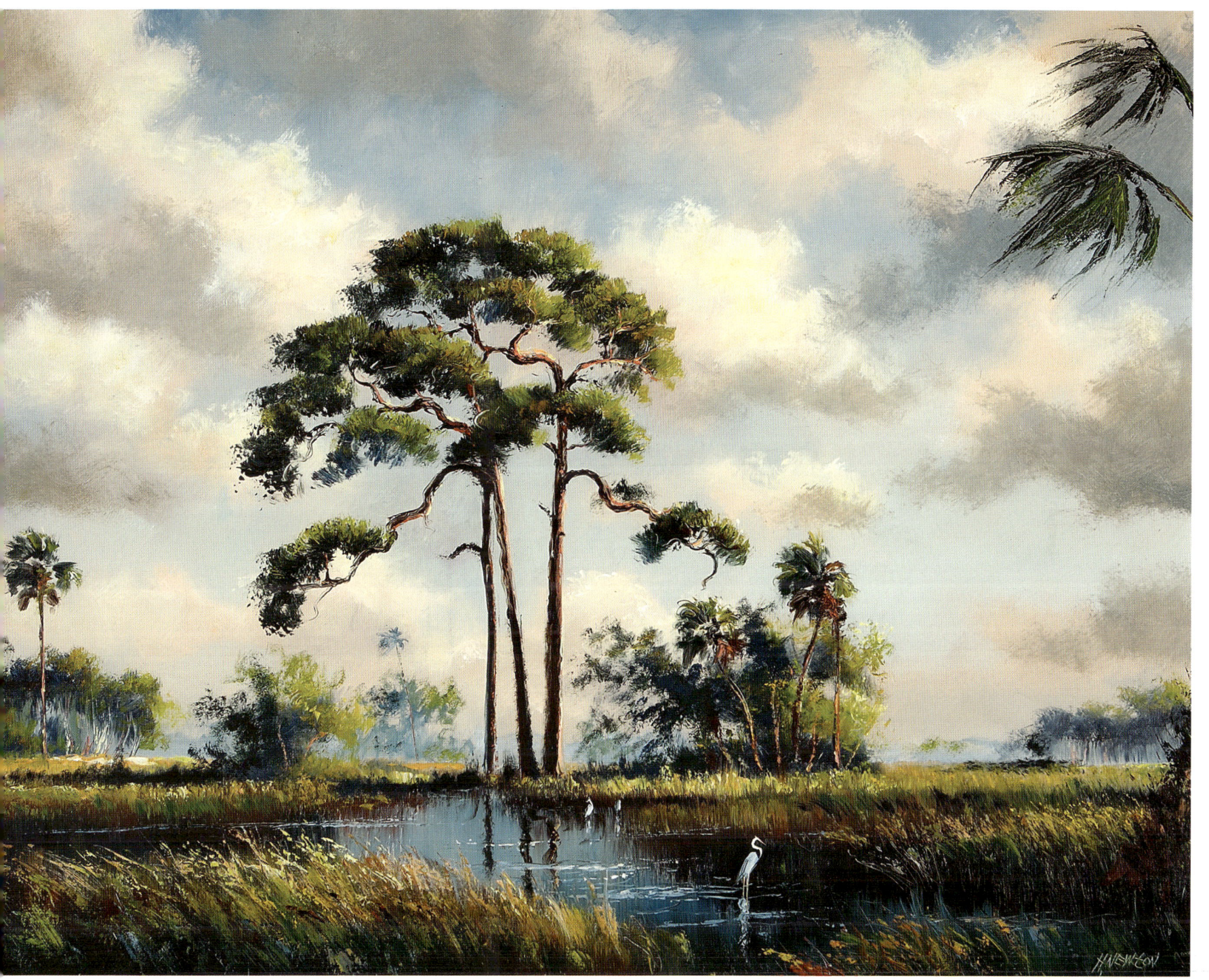

13. 15⅜" × 19½" oil on canvas board.

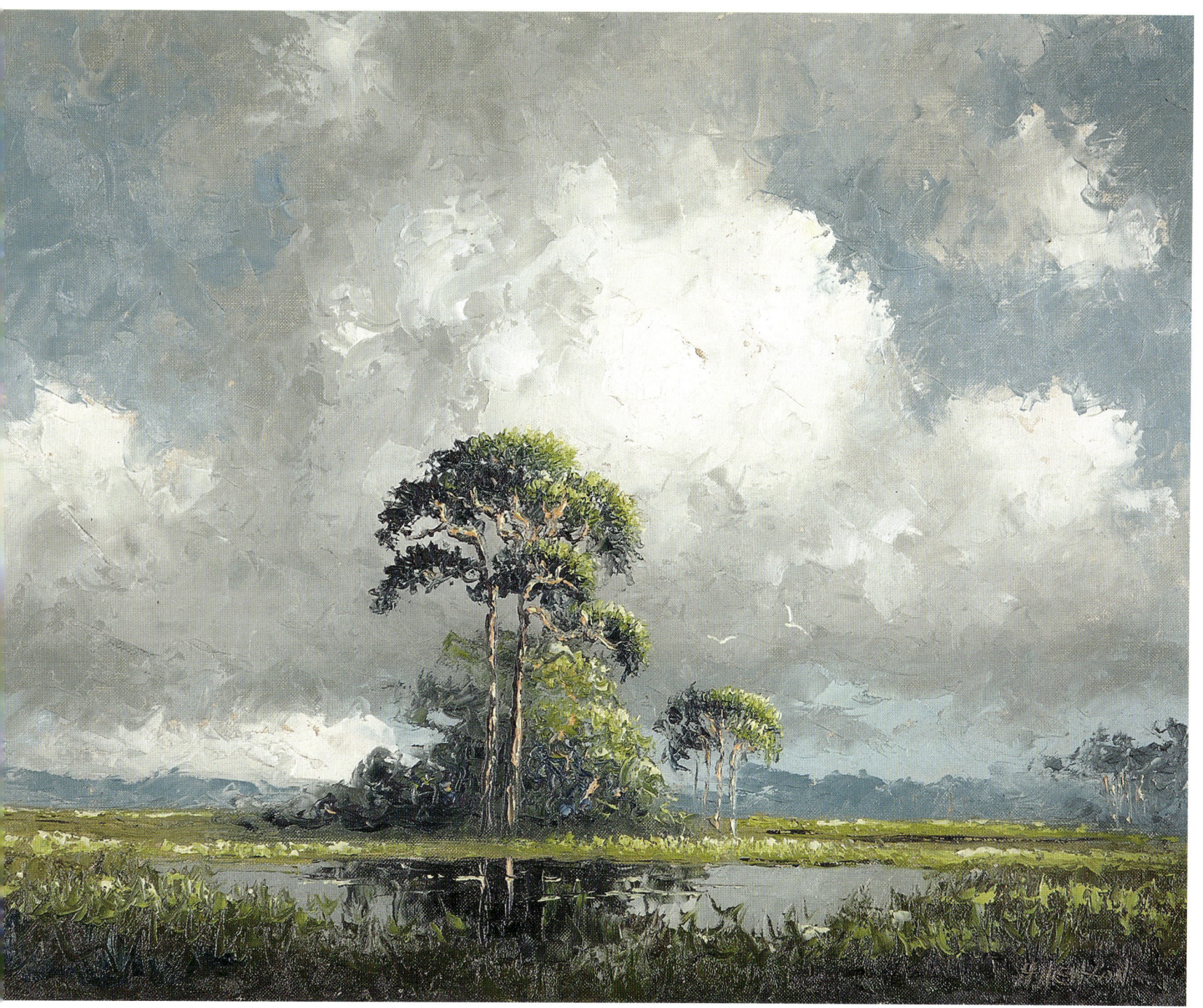

14. 29½" × 37⅝" oil on Masonite.

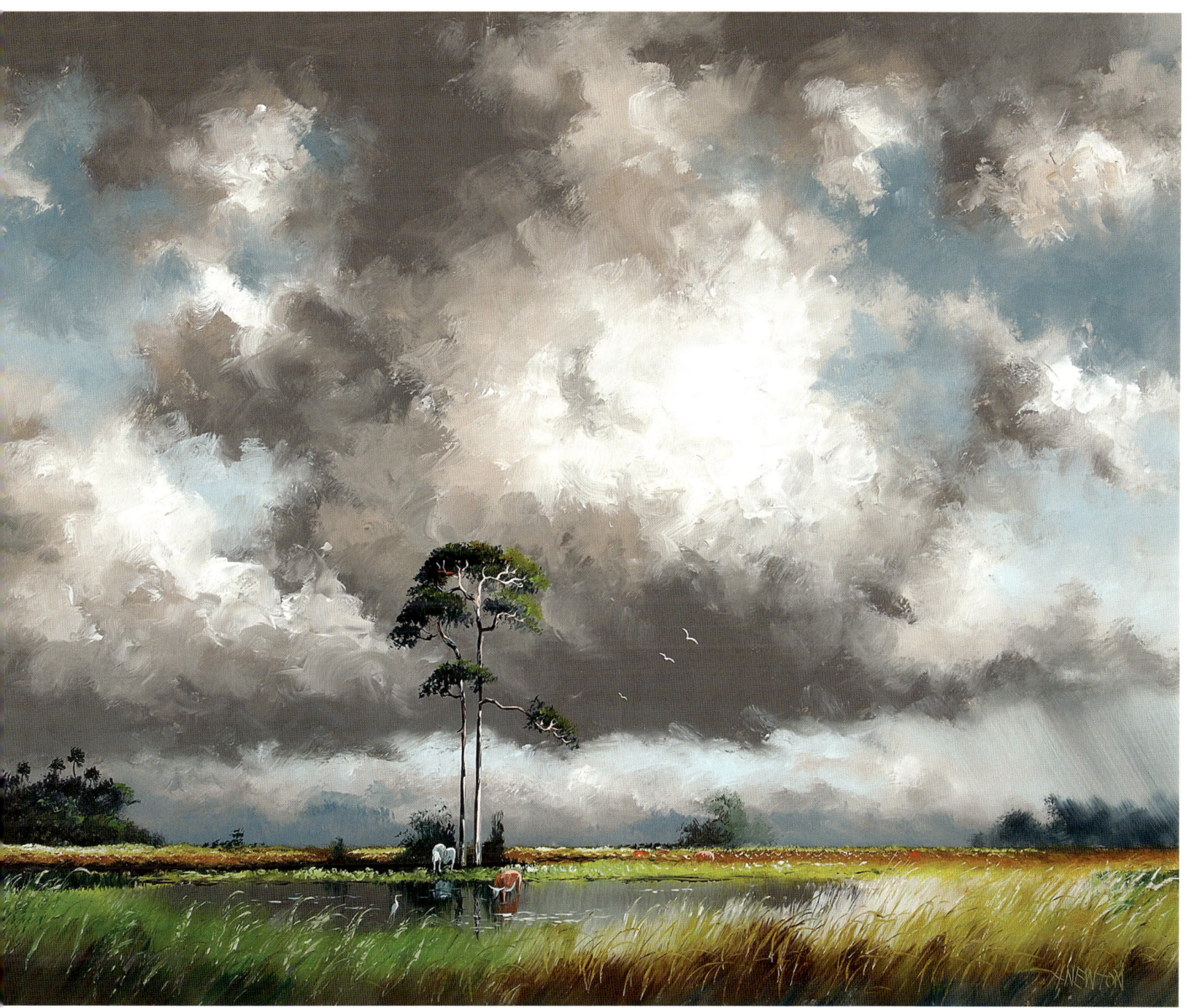

15. 15⅜" × 19½" oil on Masonite.

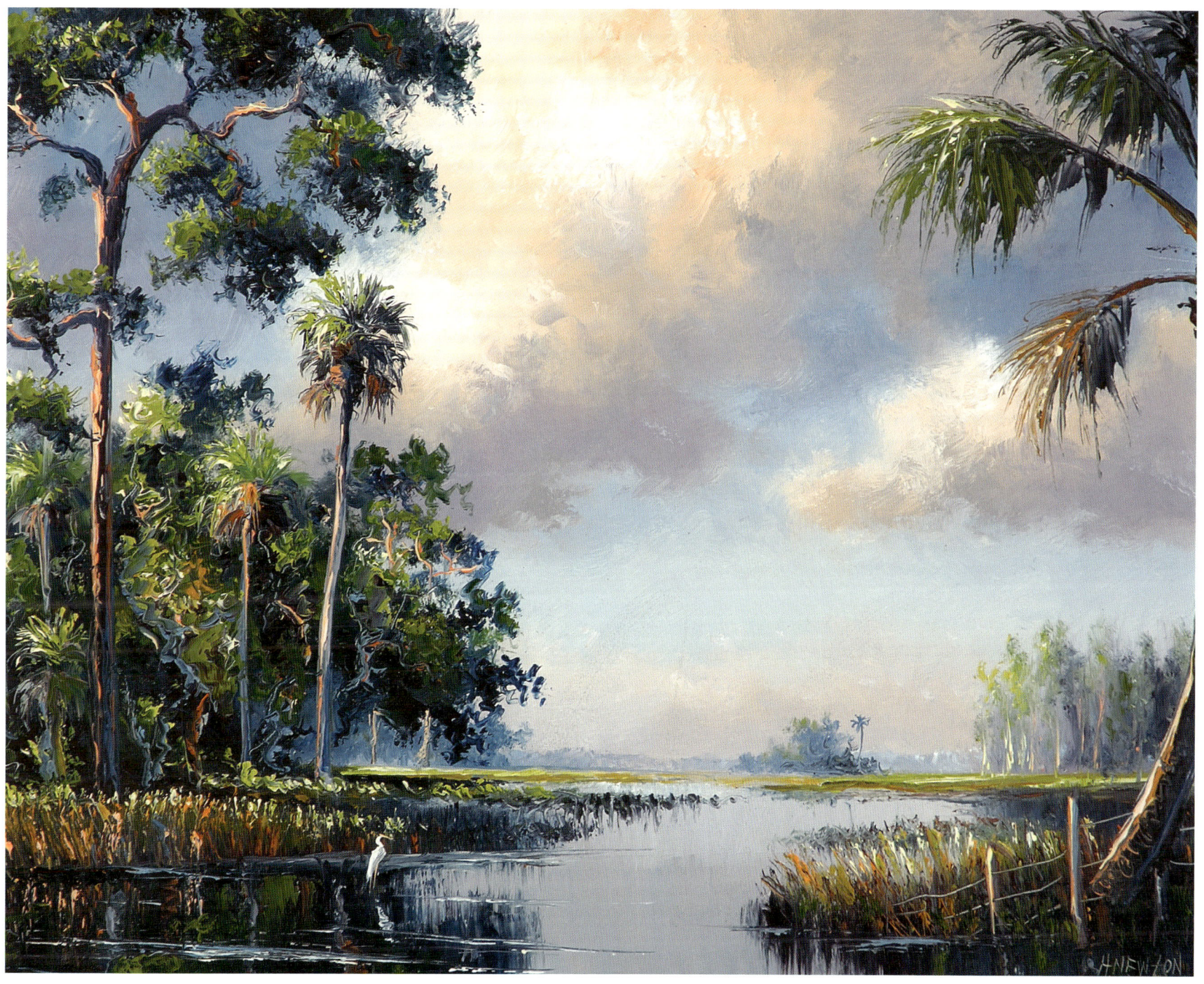

16. 17½" × 23½" oil on Masonite.

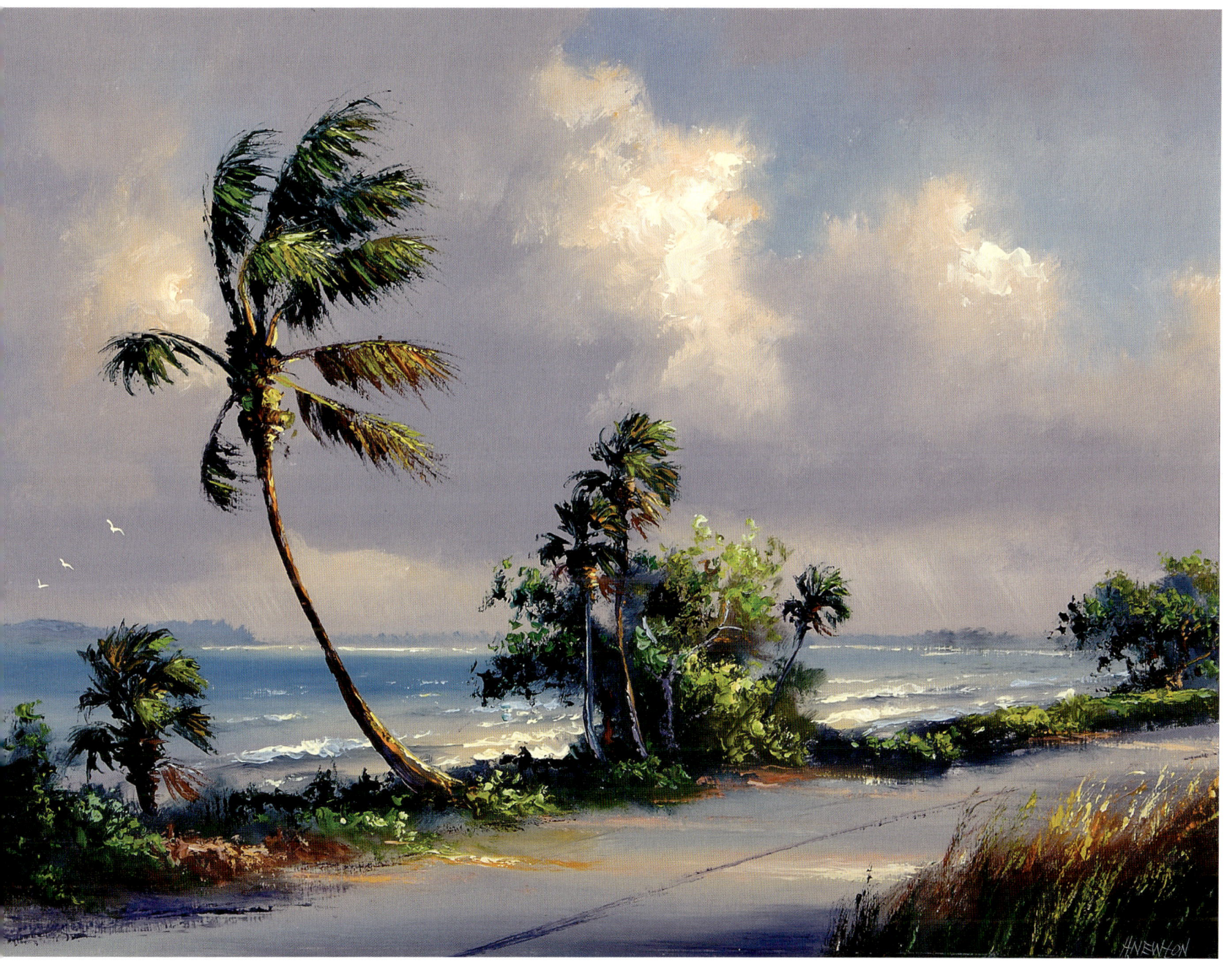

17. 21" × 29" oil on canvas board.

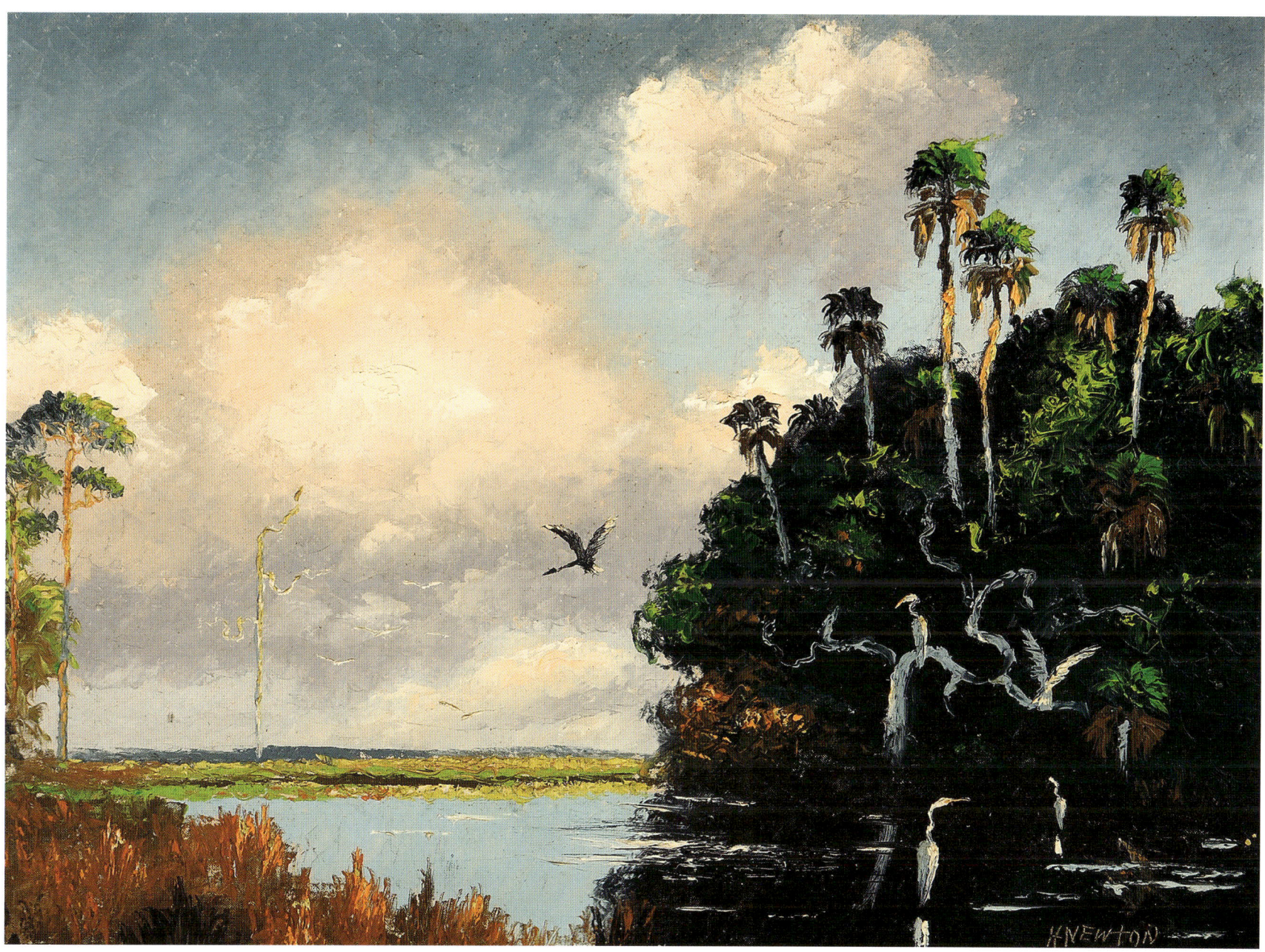

18. 21⅜" × 29⅜" oil on canvas board.

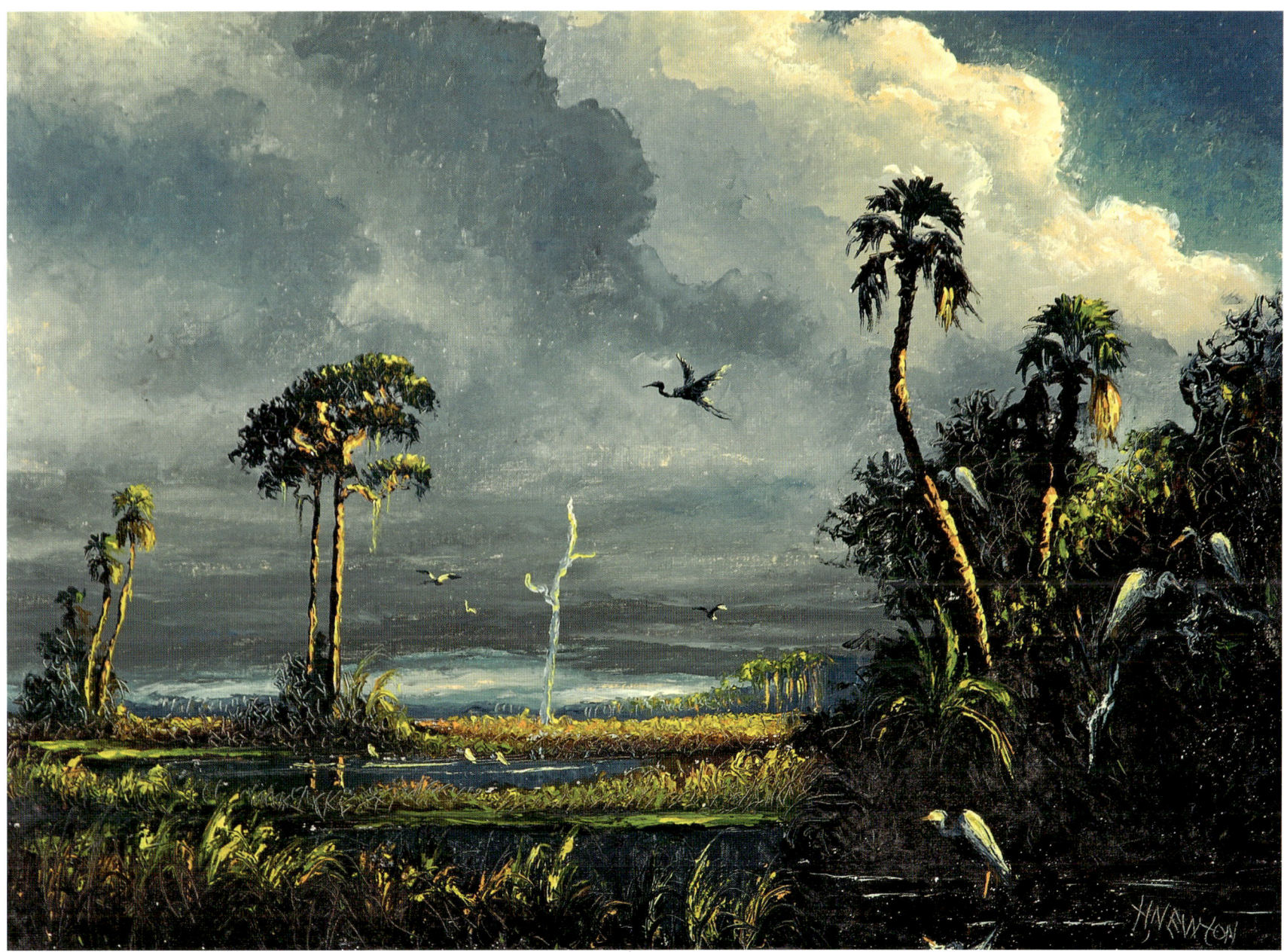

19. 19⅛" × 23" oil on canvas board.

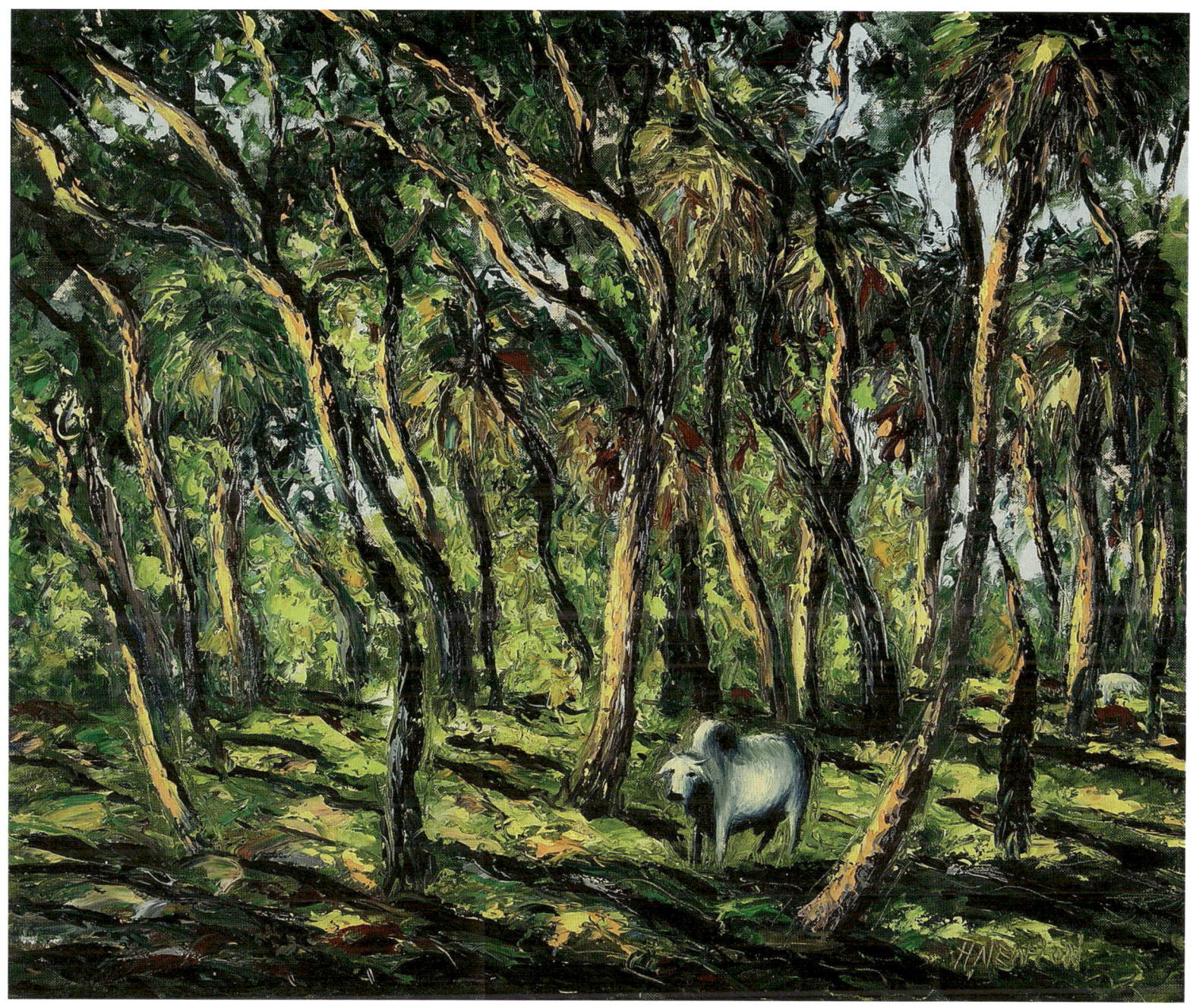

20. 23" × 28½" oil on Upson board.

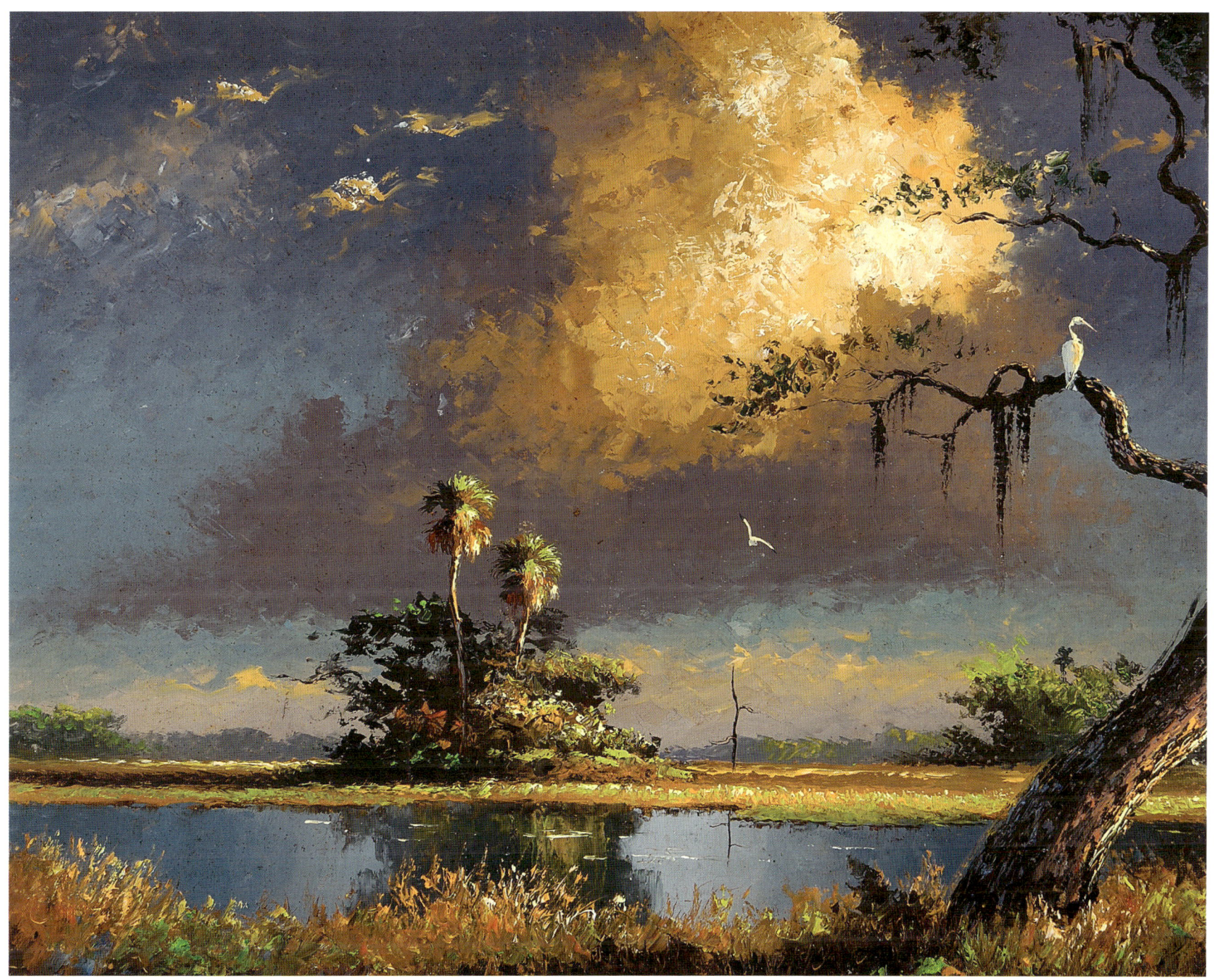

21. 15⅛" × 18⅞" oil on canvas board.

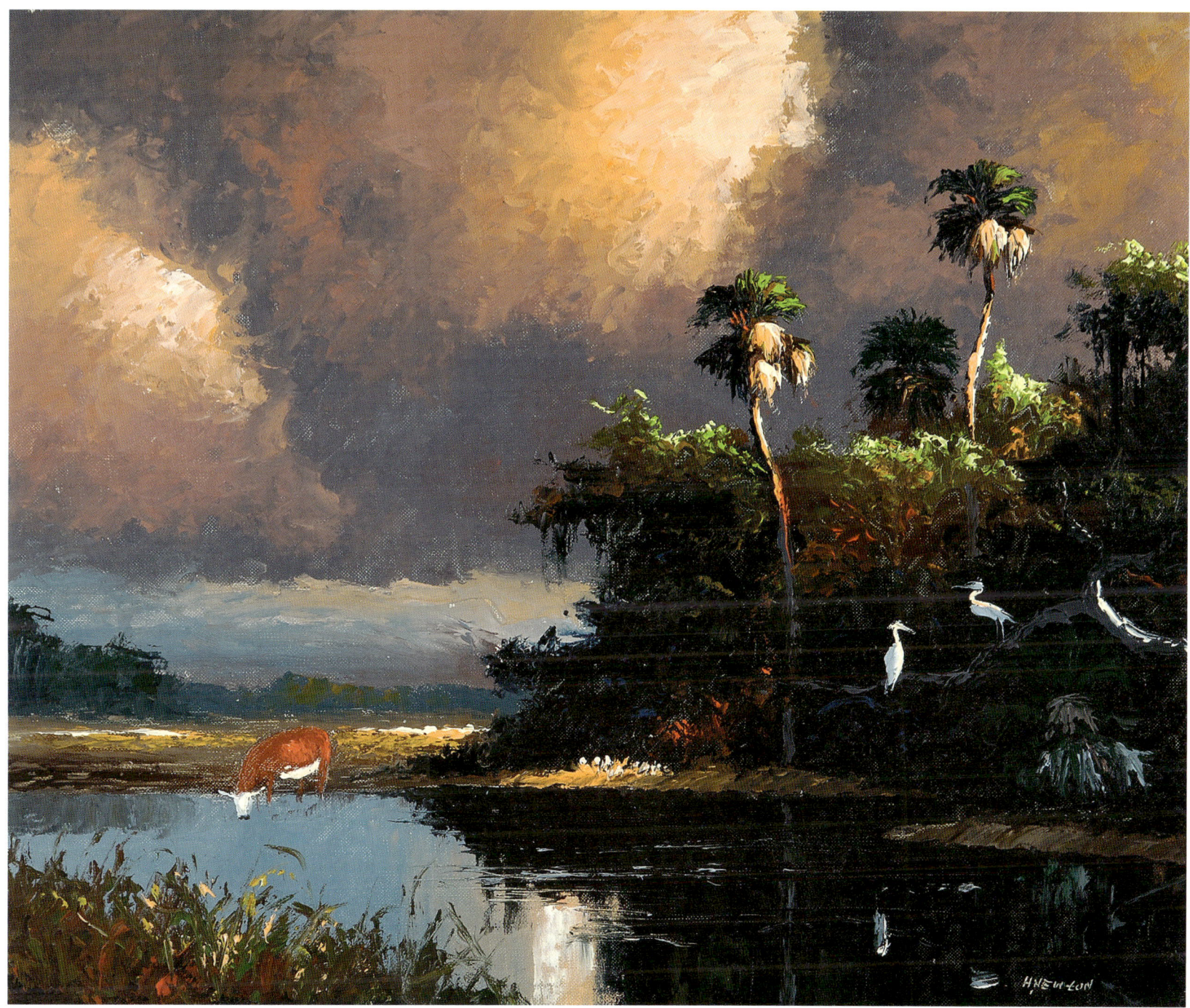

22. 23½" × 28" oil on Upson board.

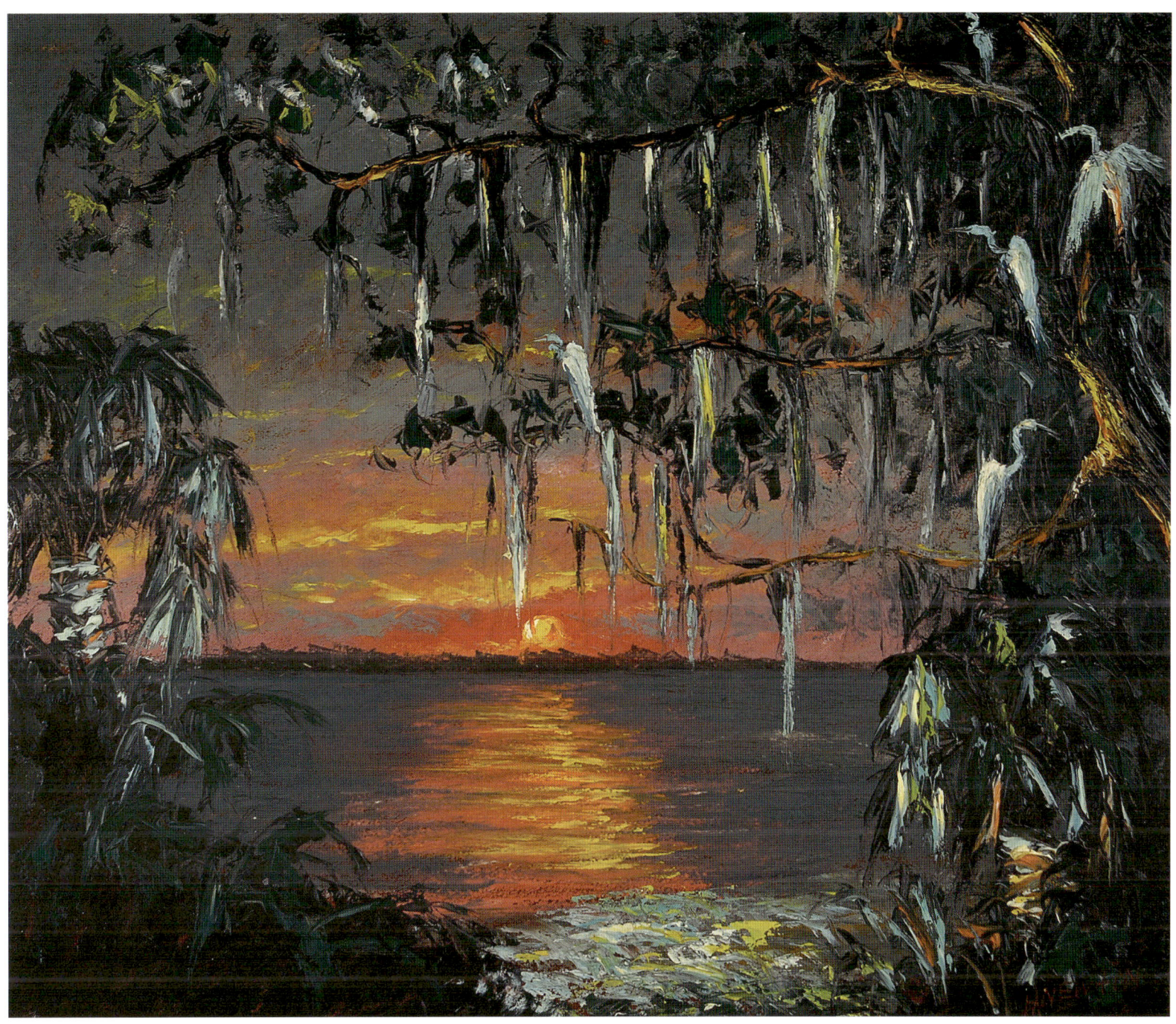

23. 16" × 20" oil on canvas board.

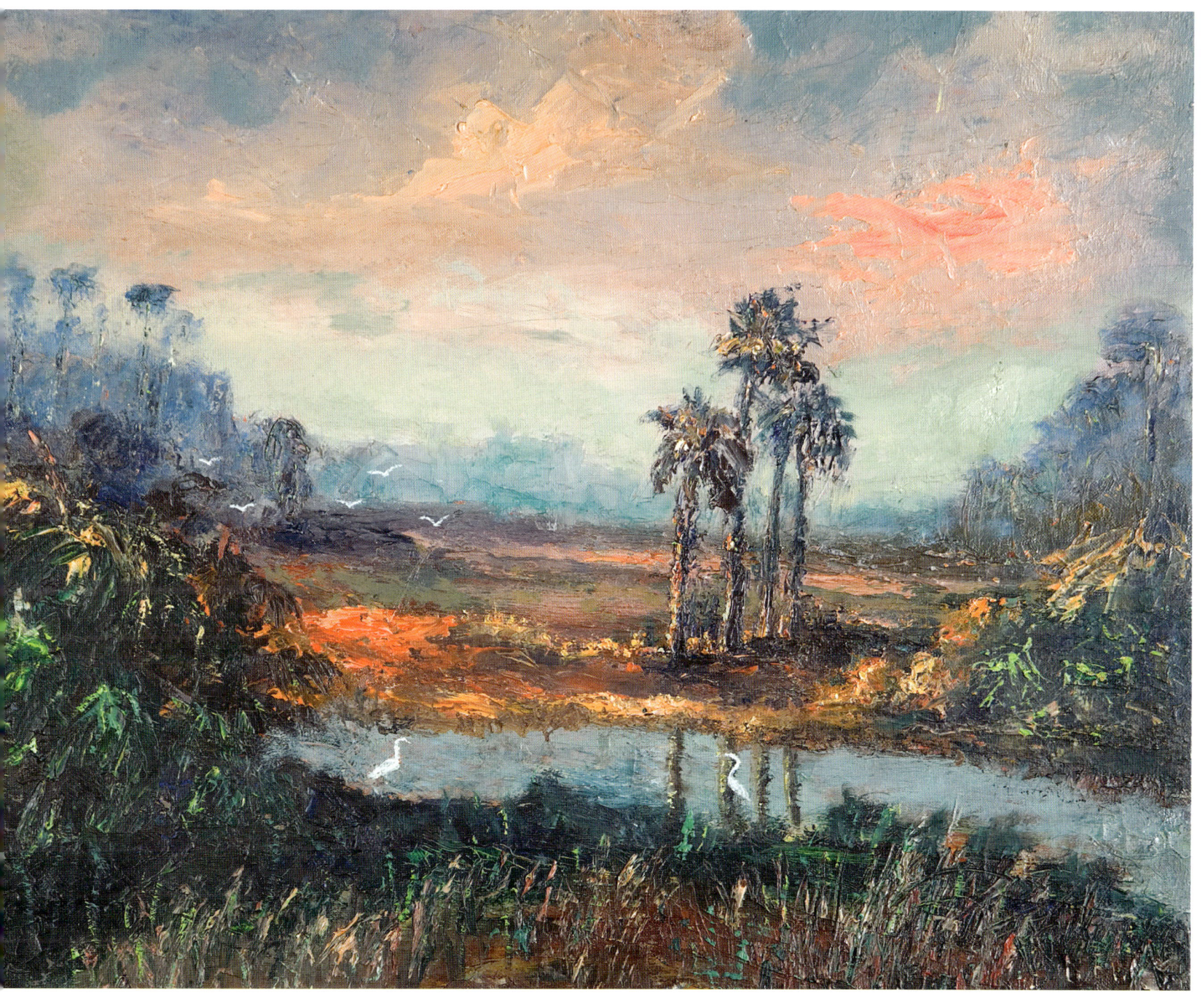

24. 35½" × 47¼" oil on Upson board.

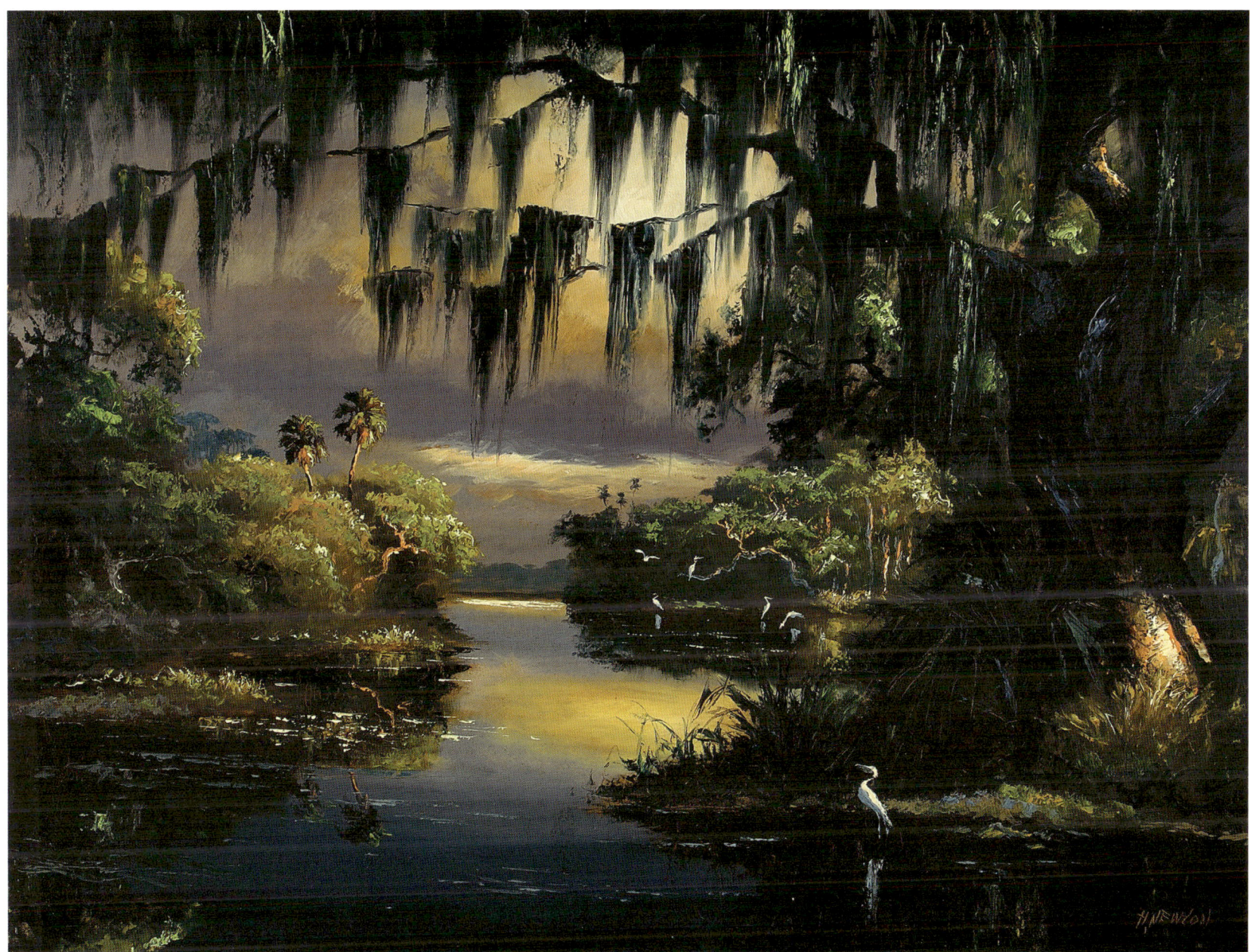

25. 23¼" × 35¼" oil on Upson board.

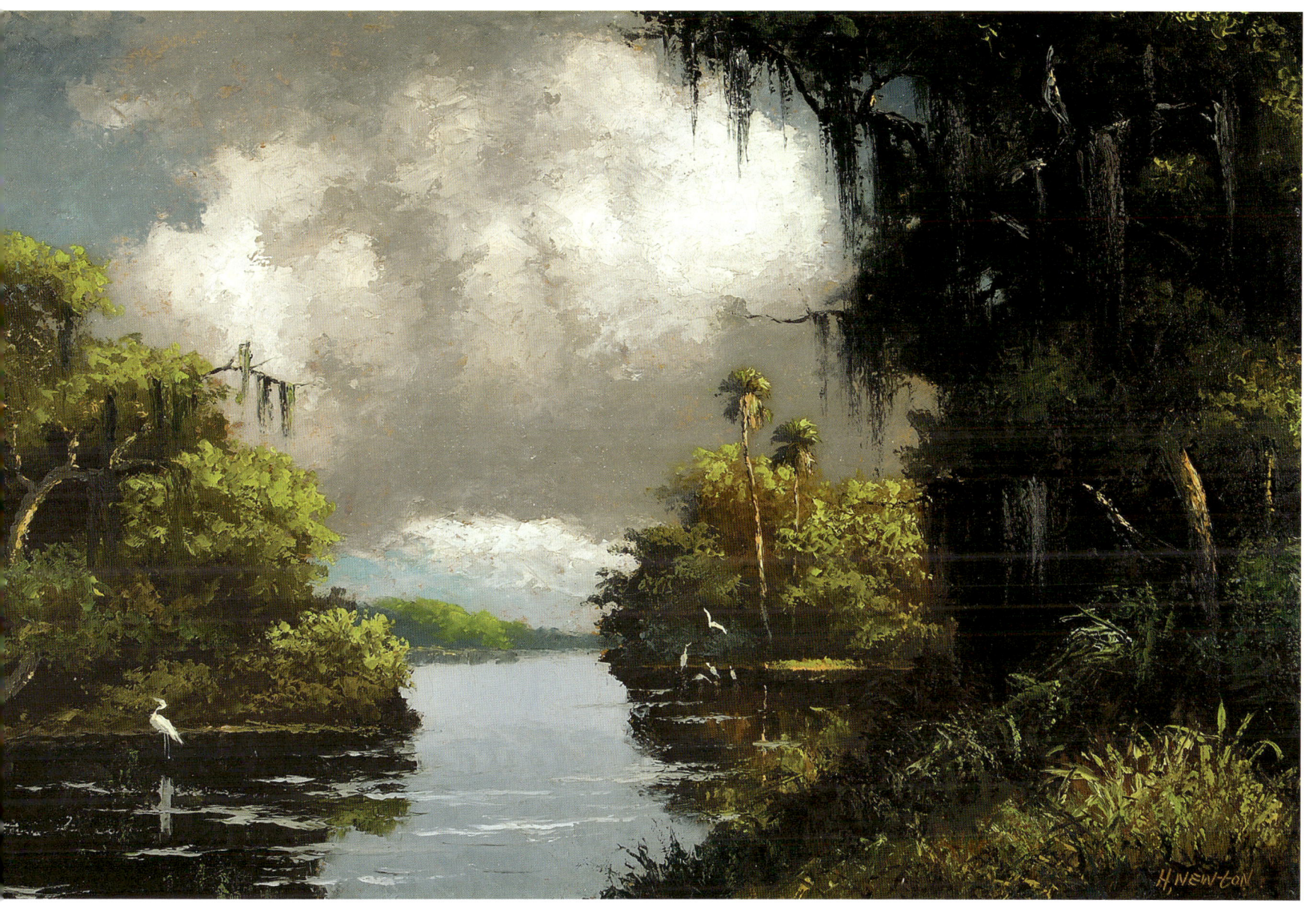

26. 23½" × 35½" oil on Upson board.

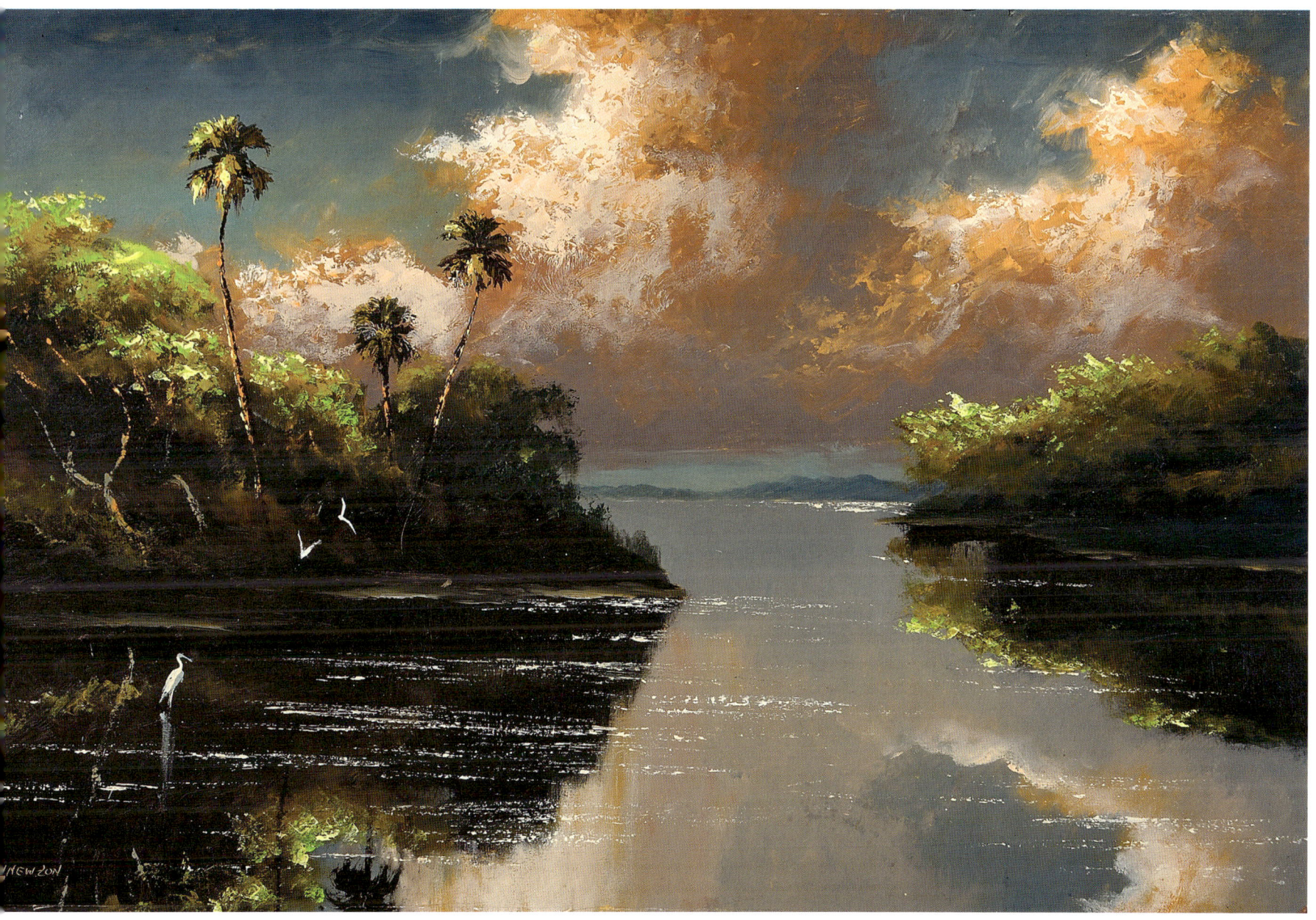

27. 19⅜" × 23⅜" oil on canvas board.

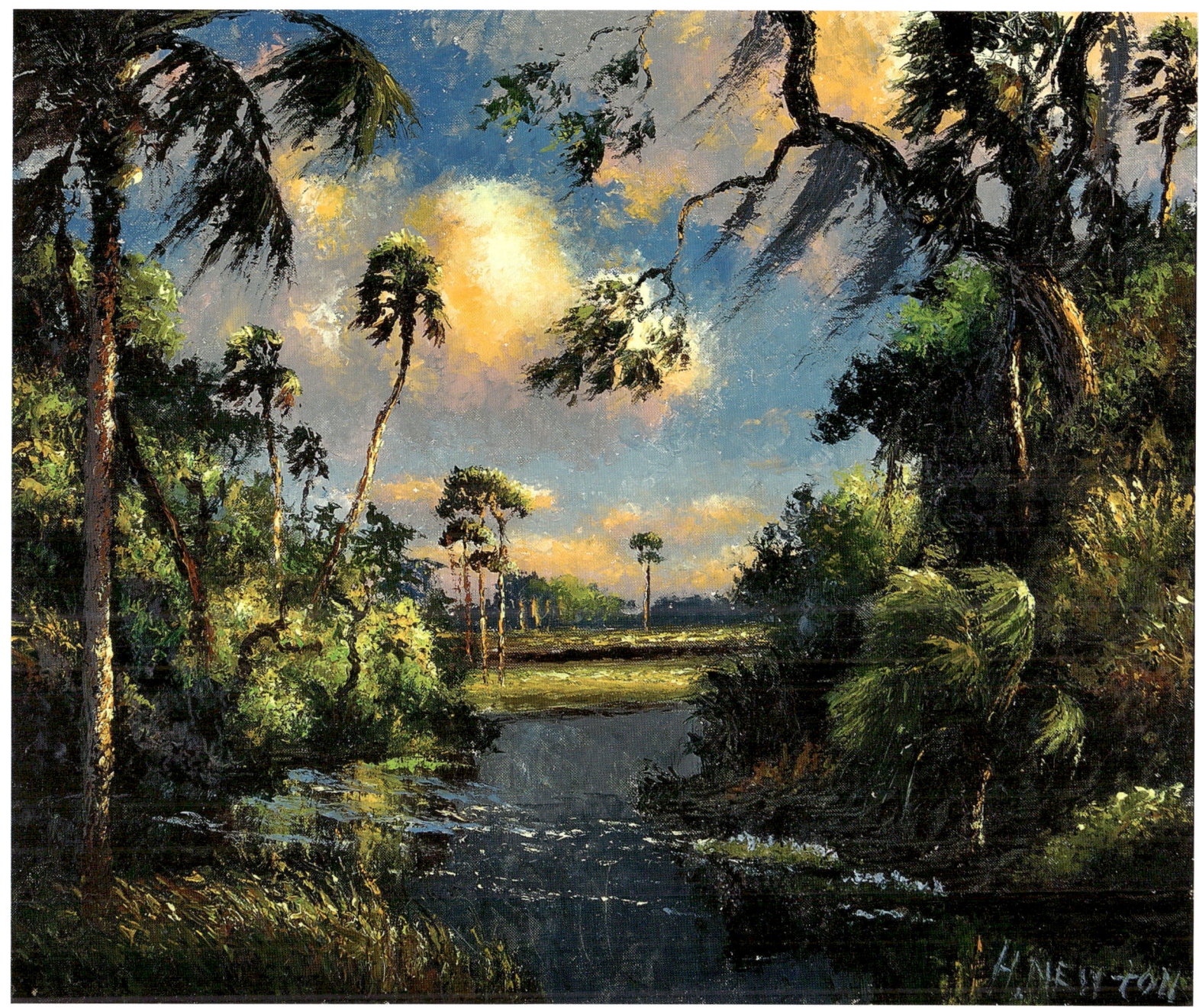

28. 22¾" × 19" oil on canvas board.

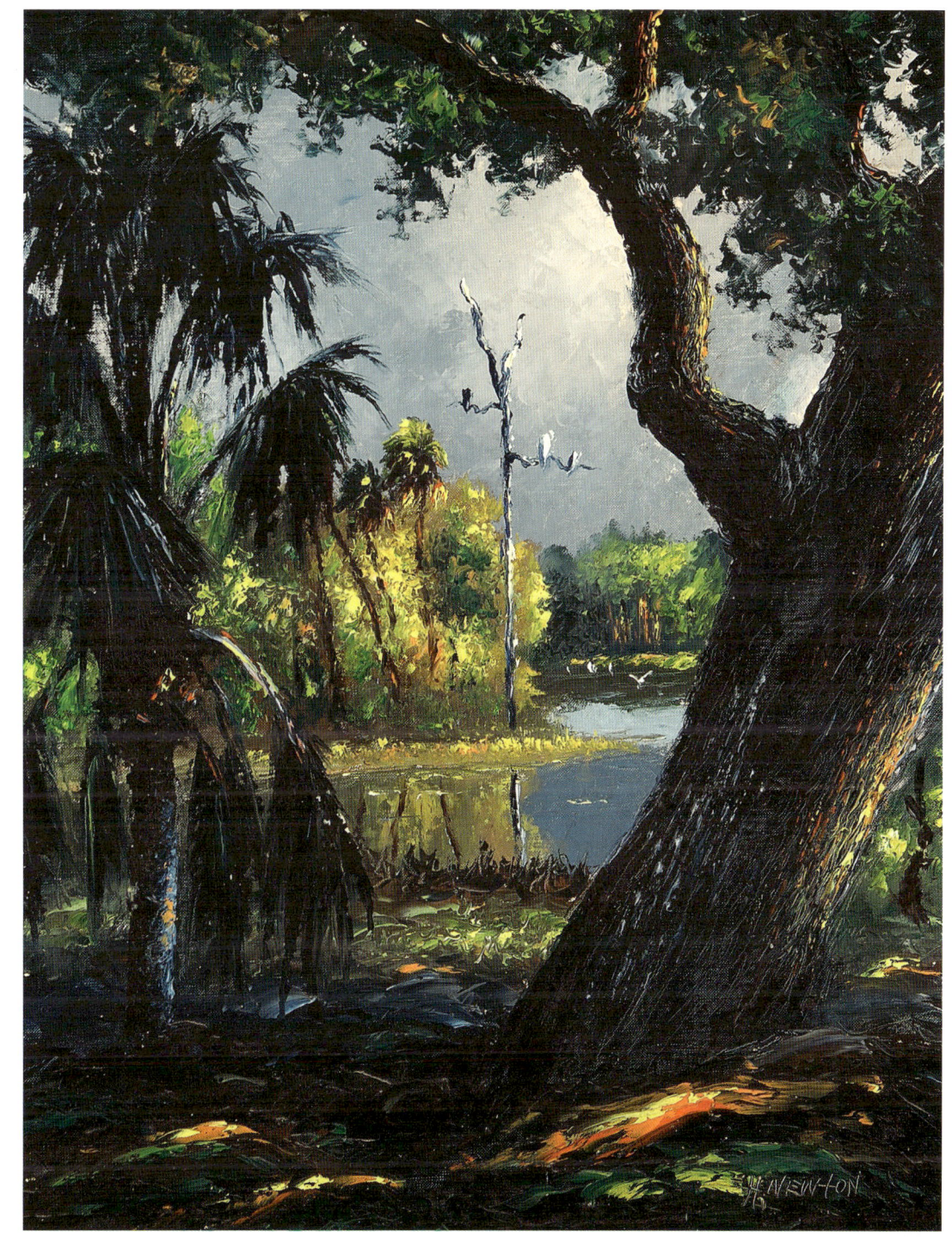

29. 23¼" × 17¼" oil on canvas board.

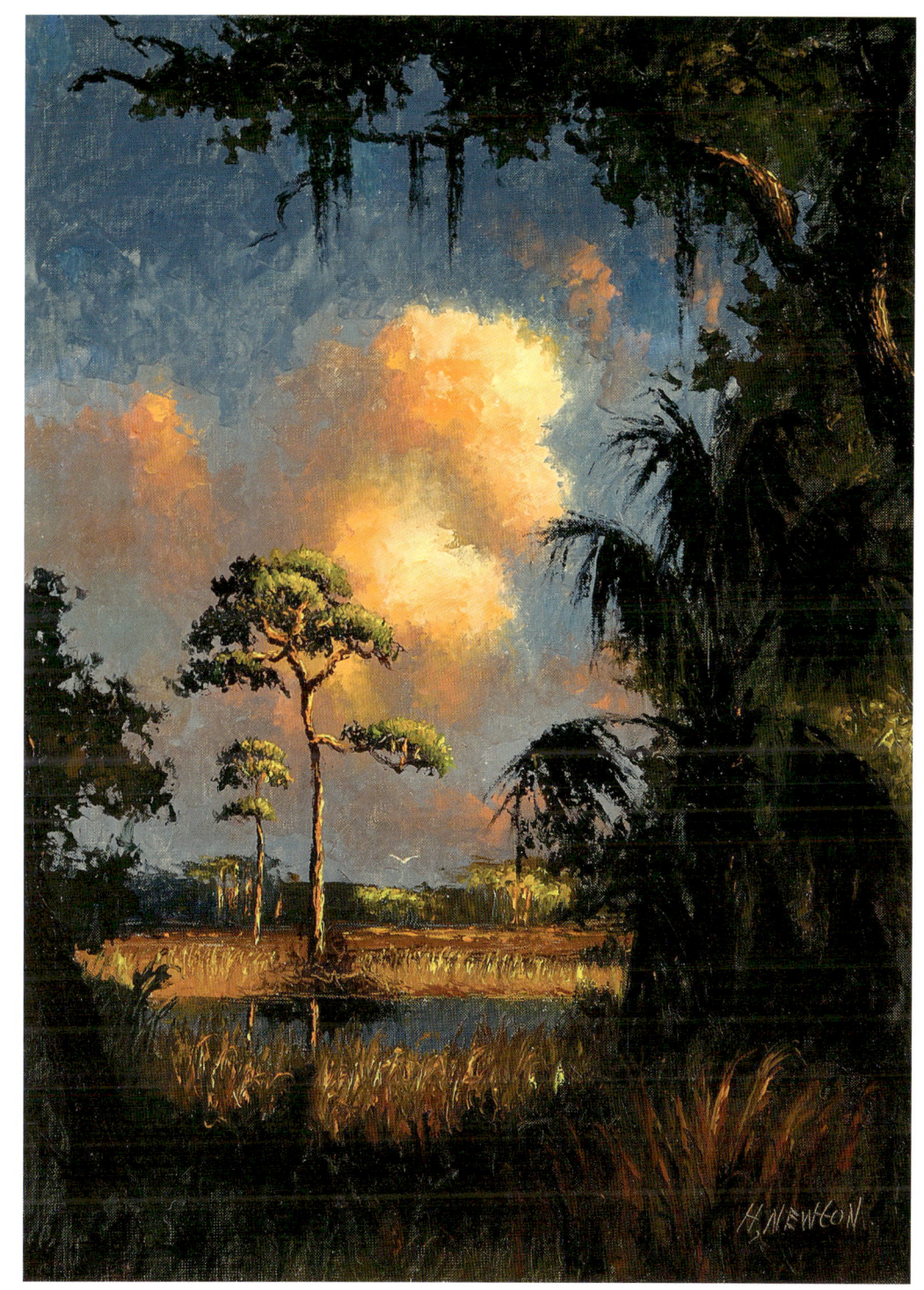

30. 20⅛" × 22½" oil on Upson board.

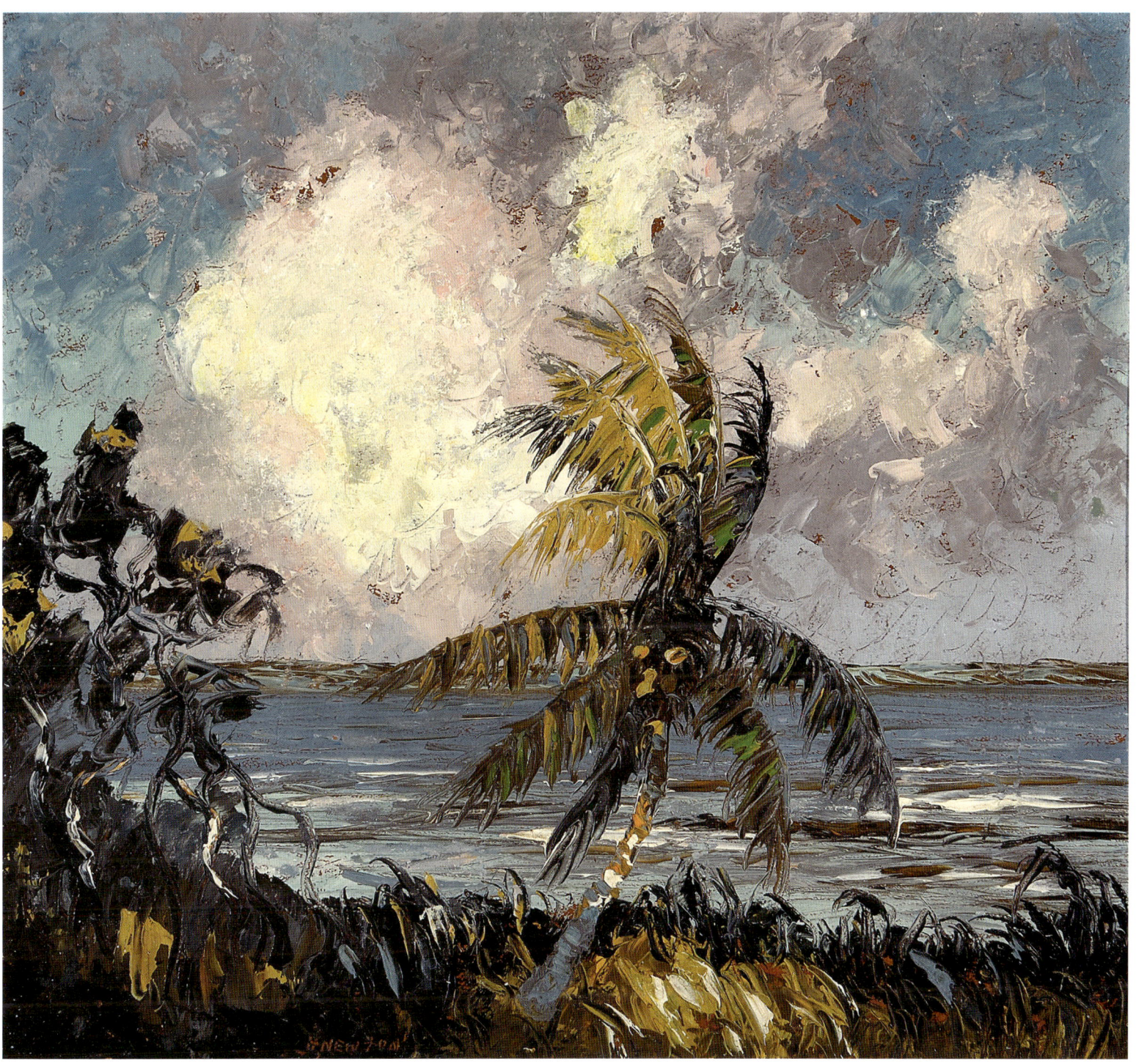

31. 23½" × 19½" oil on canvas board.

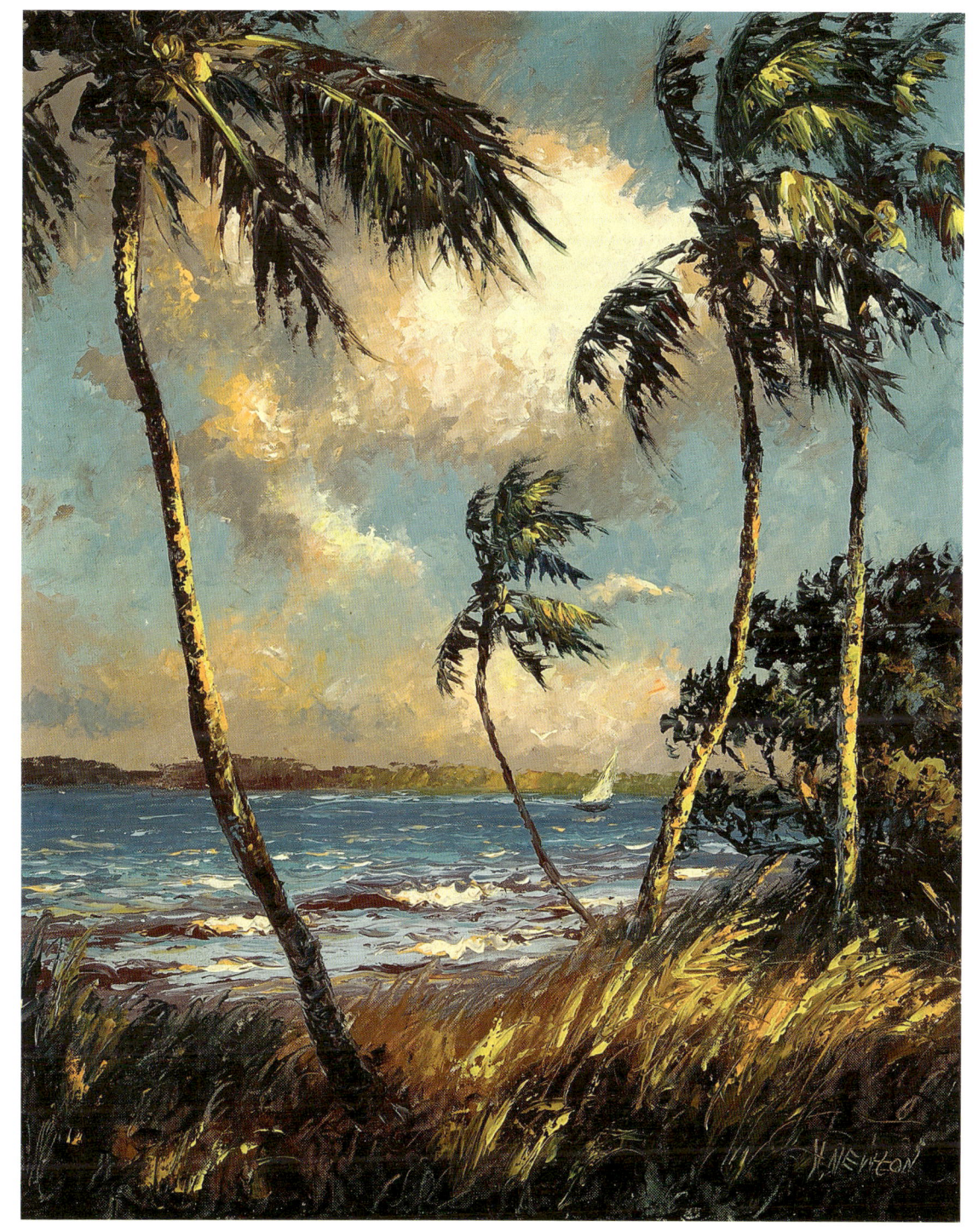

32. 21½" × 29½" oil on canvas board.

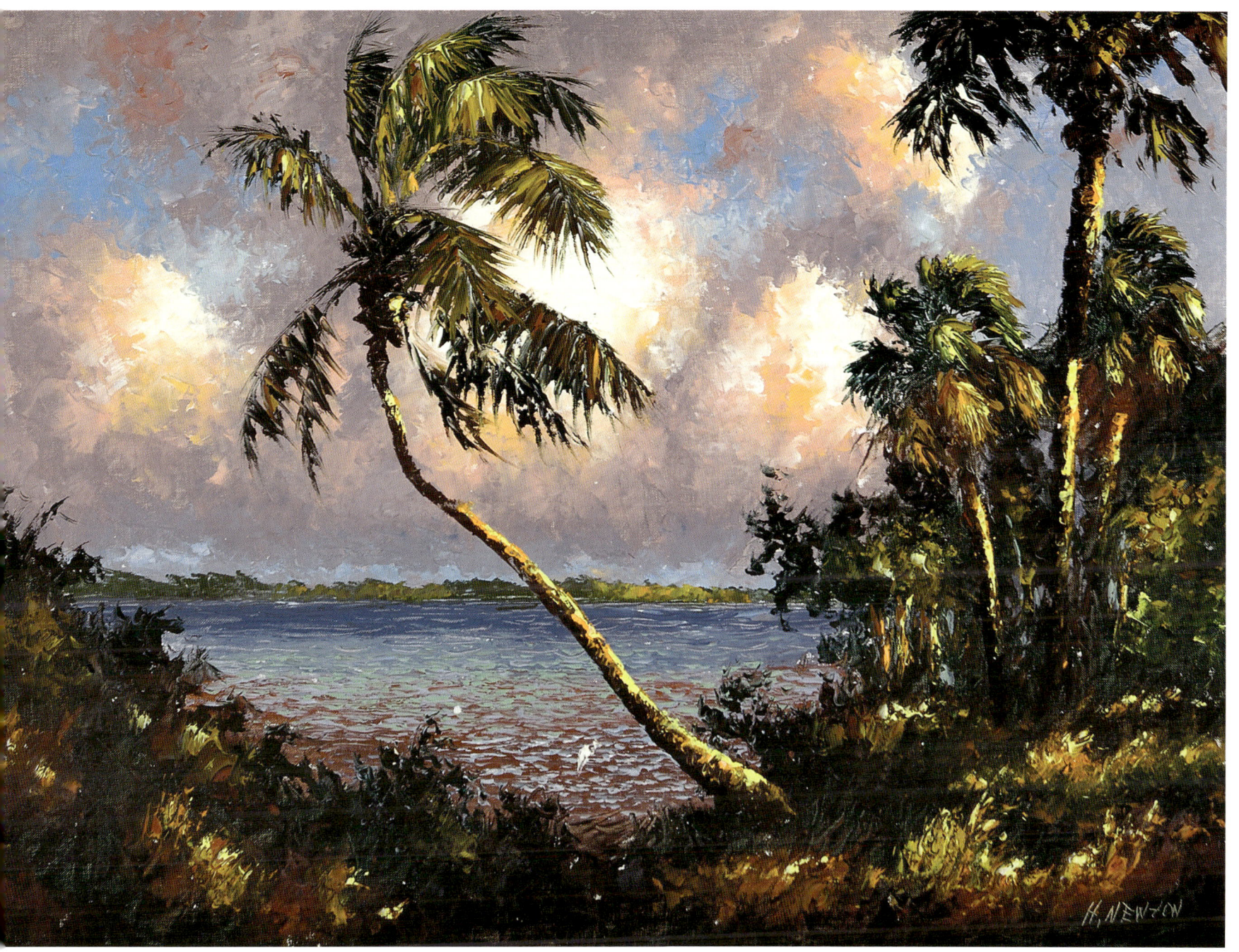

H. NEWTON

33. 13½" × 17½" oil on canvas board.

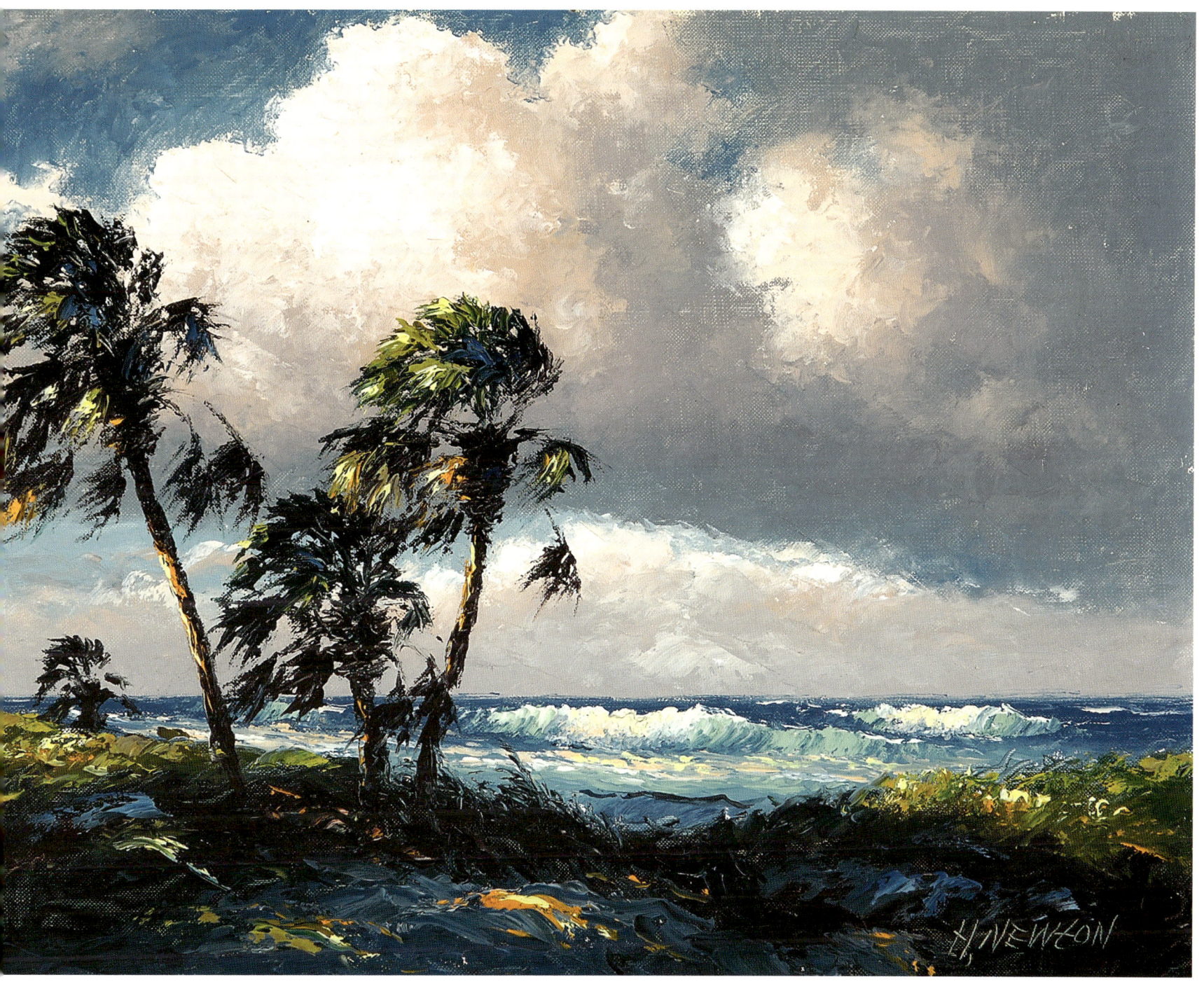

34. 17¼" × 23¼" oil on canvas board.

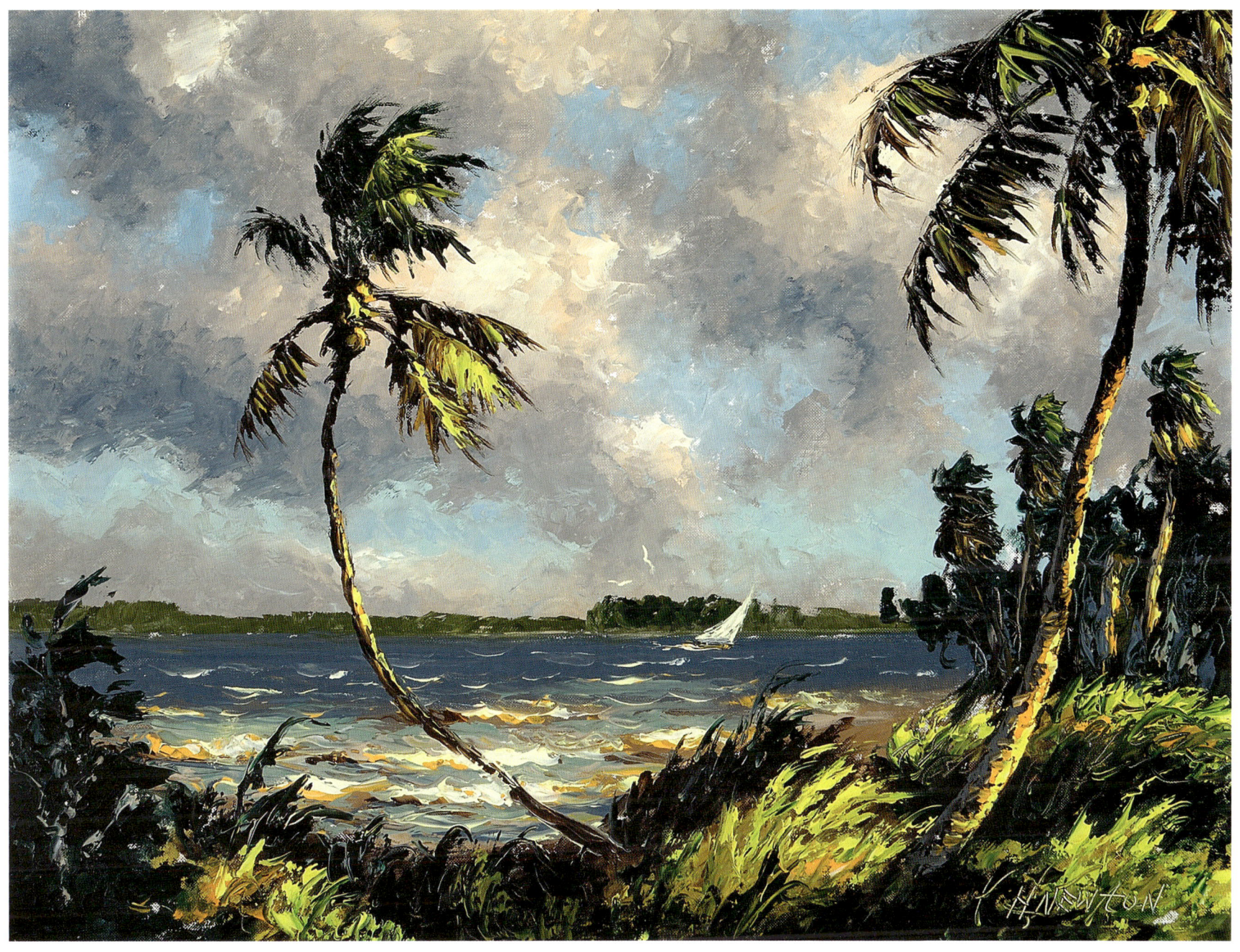

35. 21⅛″ × 29½″ oil on canvas board.

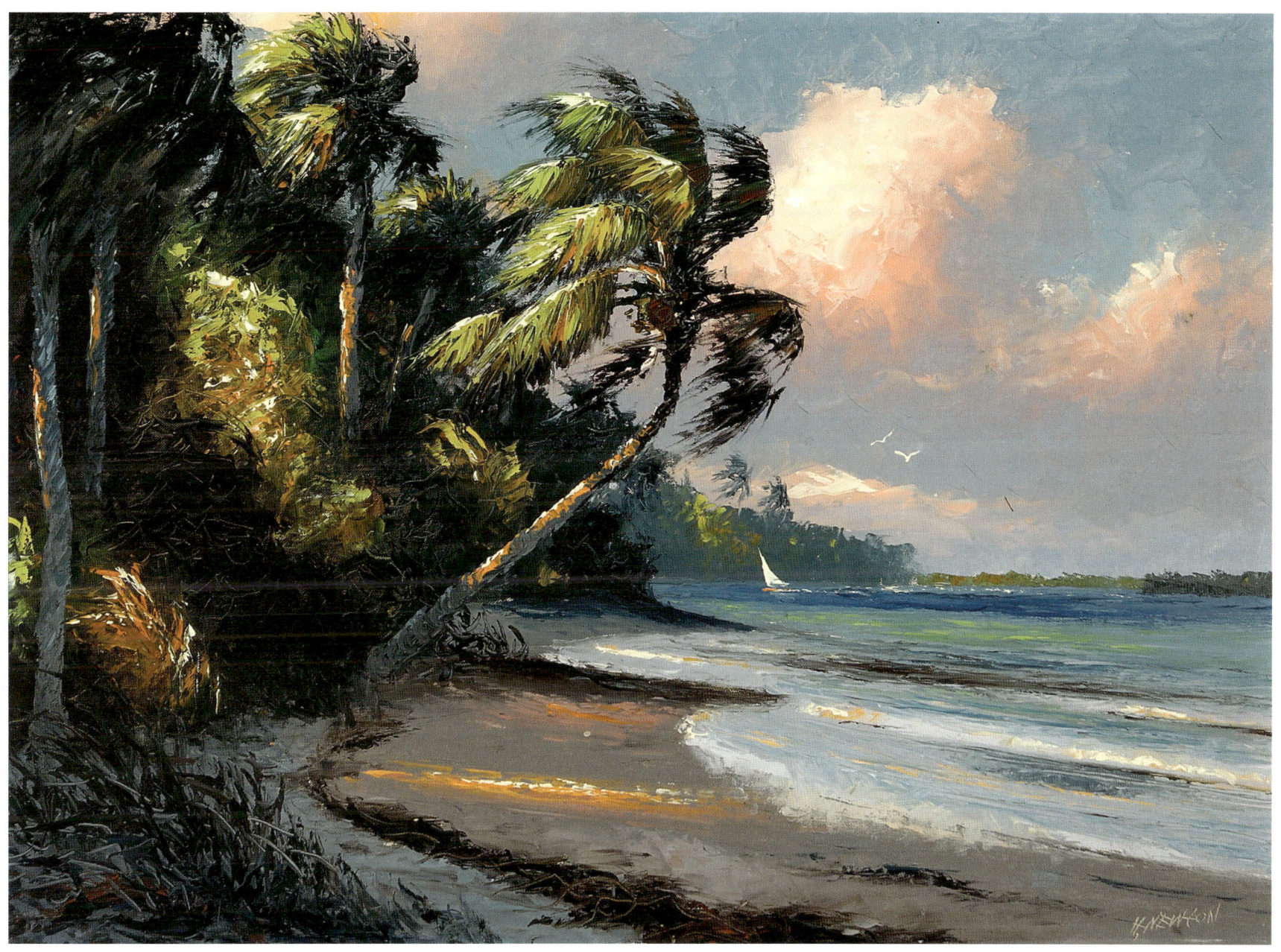

36. 20" × 29" oil on Masonite.

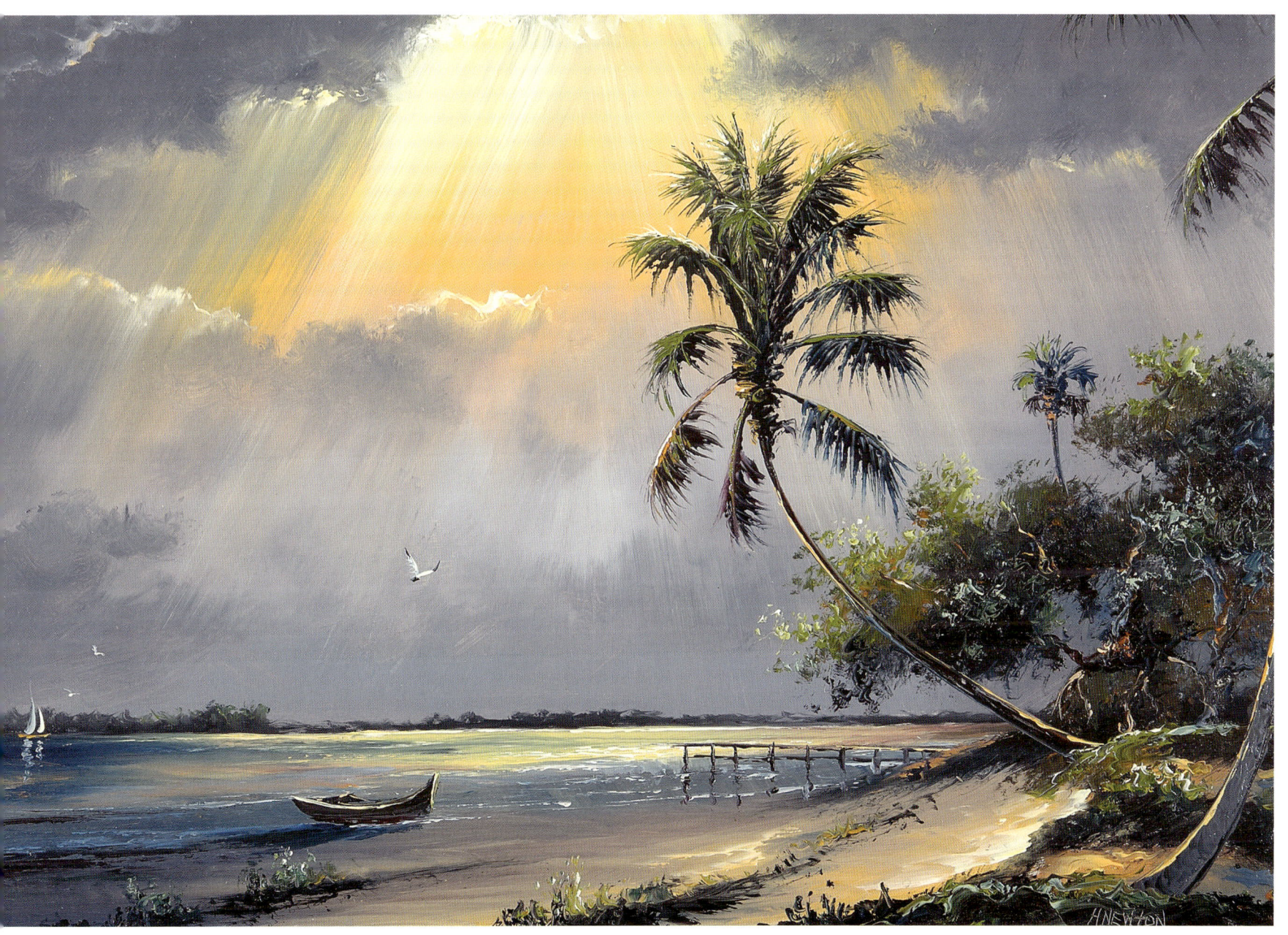

37. 22½" × 17¼" oil on Masonite.

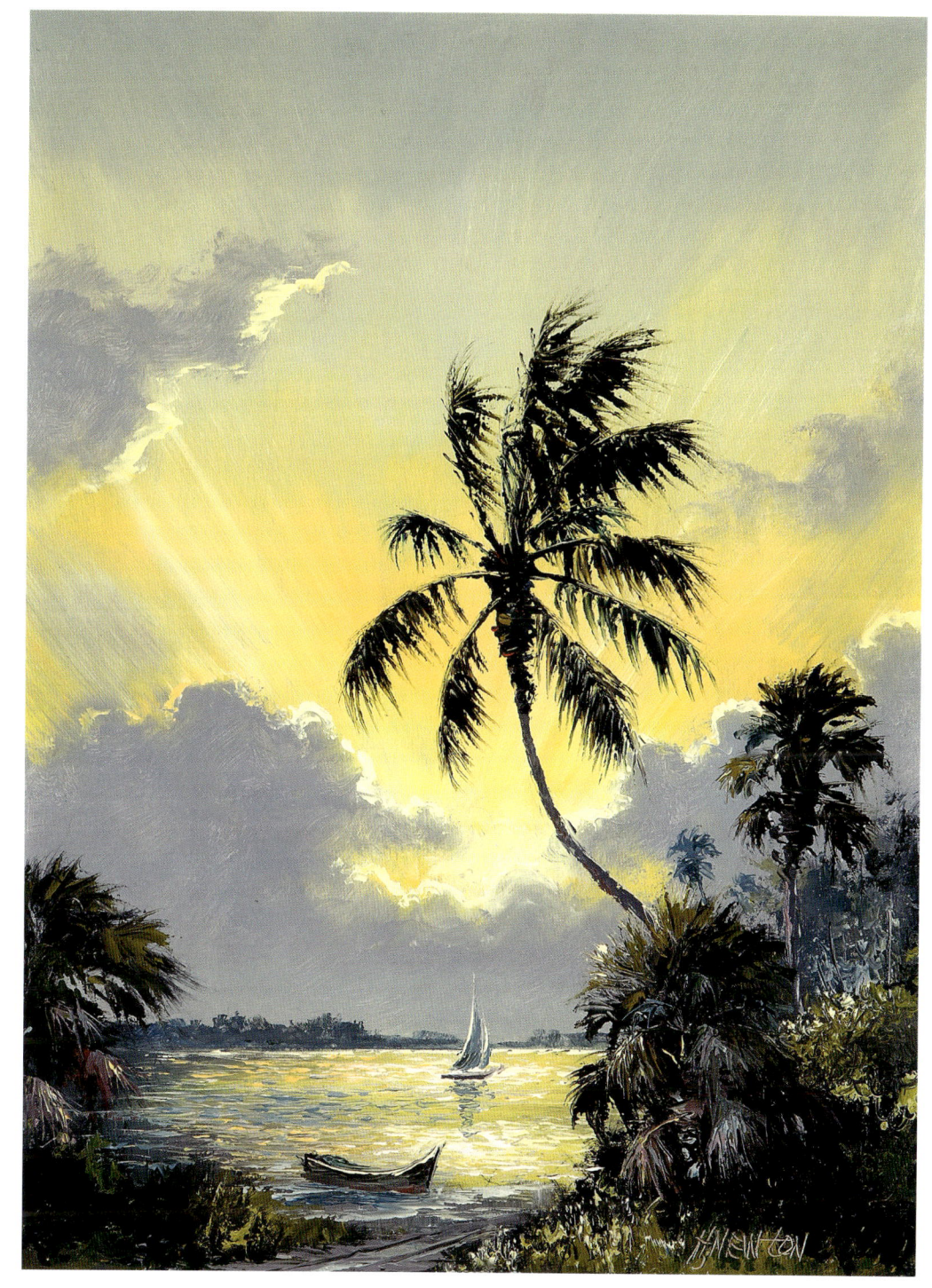

38. 15½" × 11½" oil on Masonite.

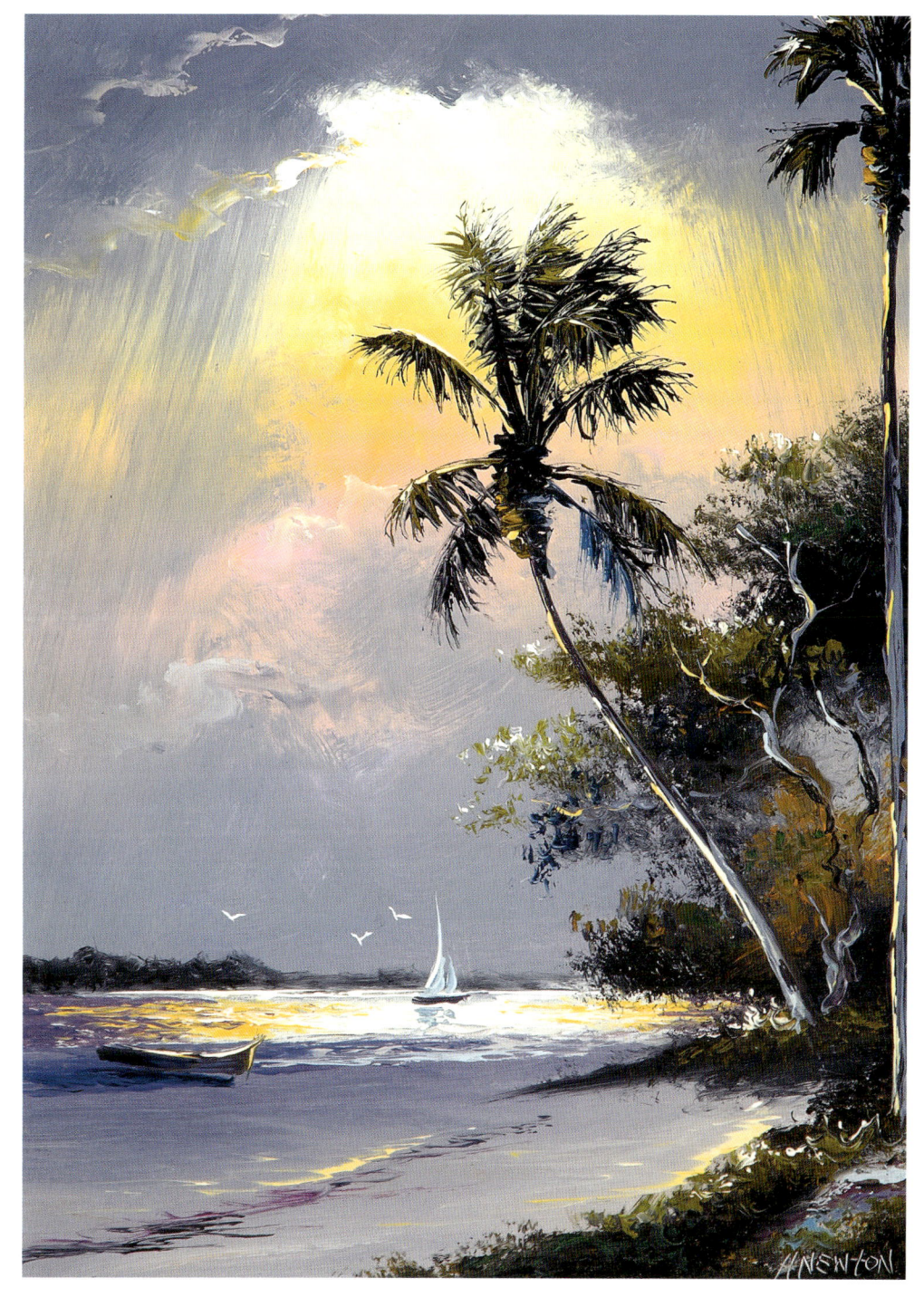

39. 23⅝" × 39½" oil on Masonite.

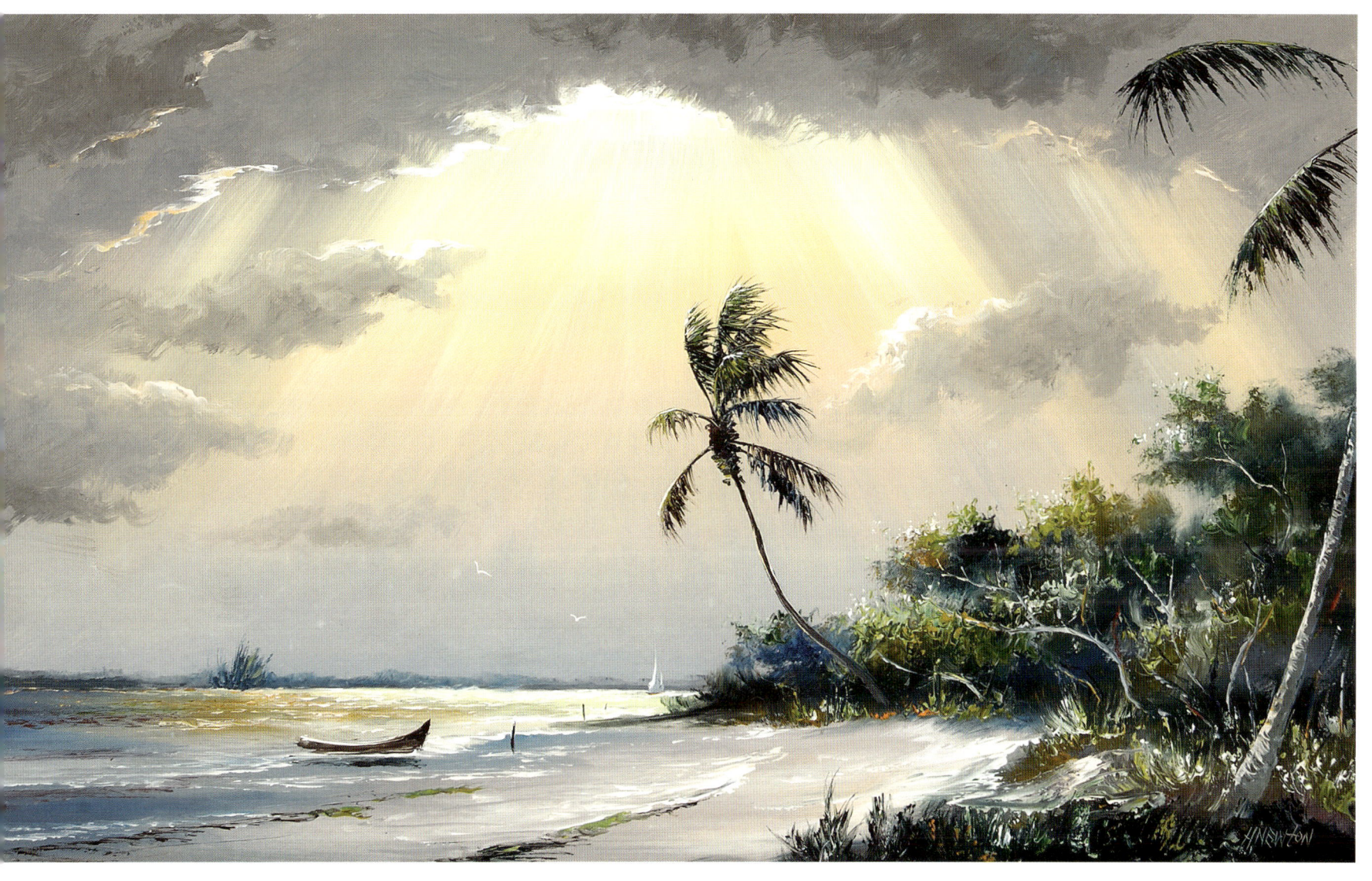

40. 24" × 18" oil on canvas board.

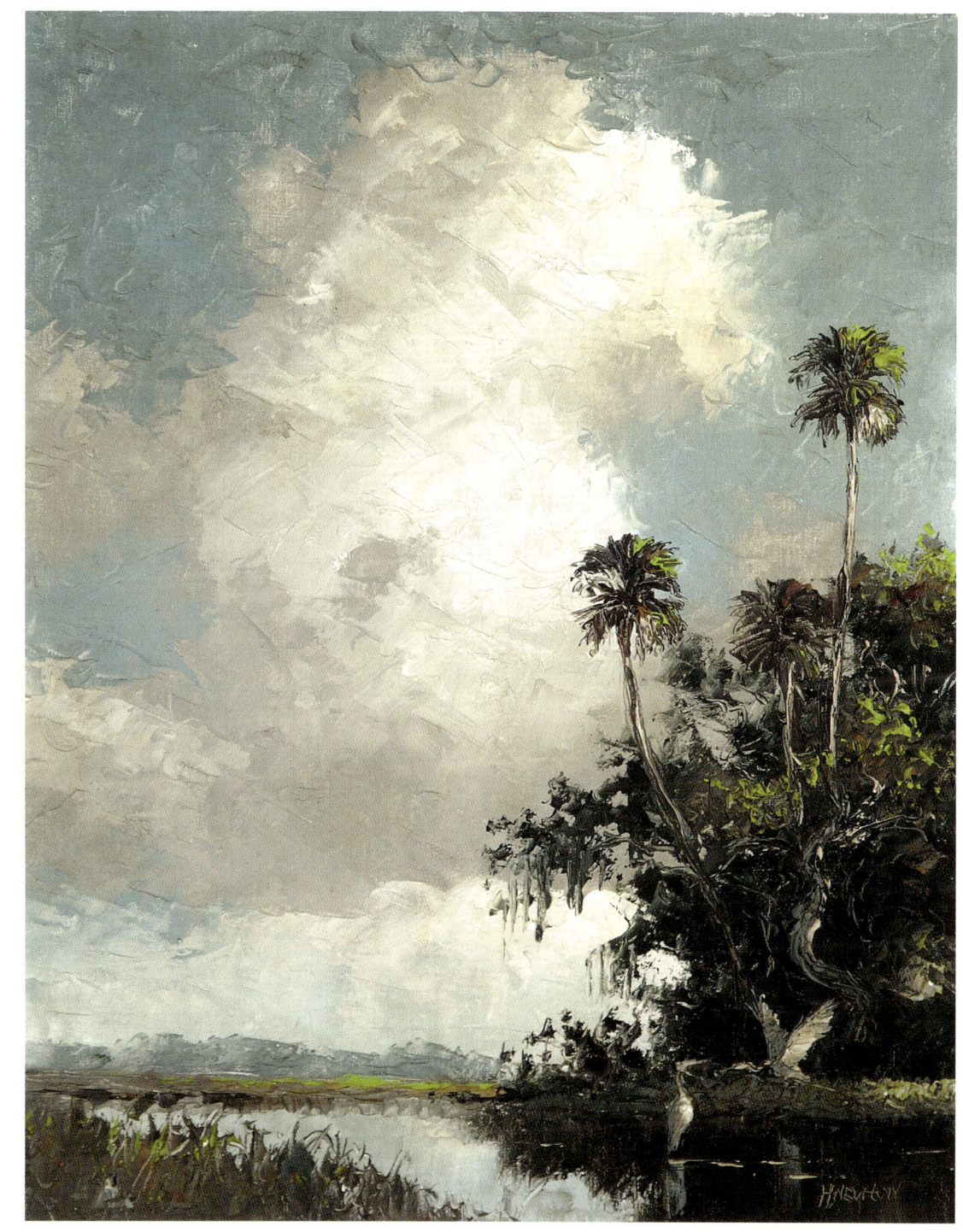

41. 23½" × 35½" oil on Masonite.

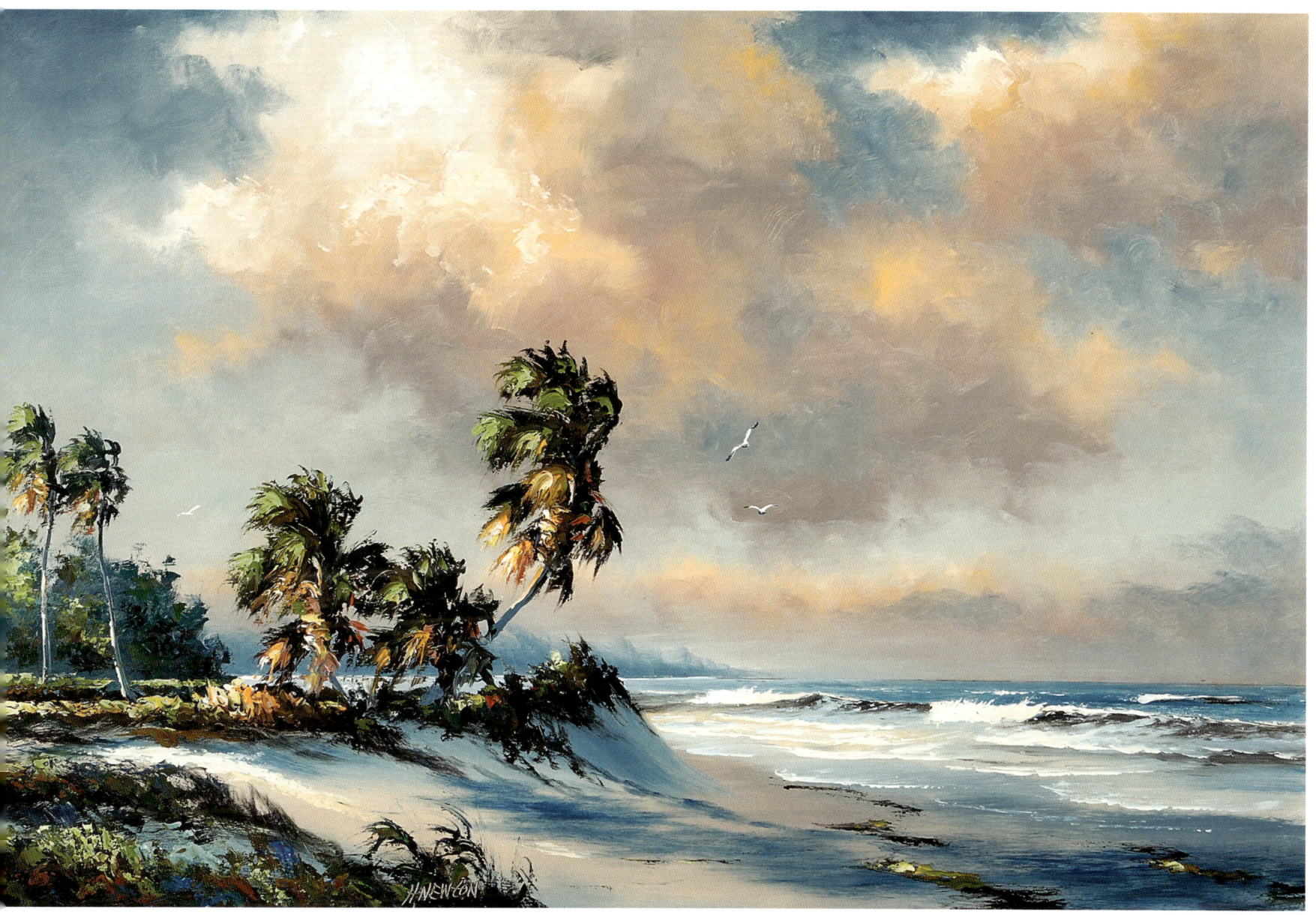

42. 26¼" × 38" oil on stretched canvas.

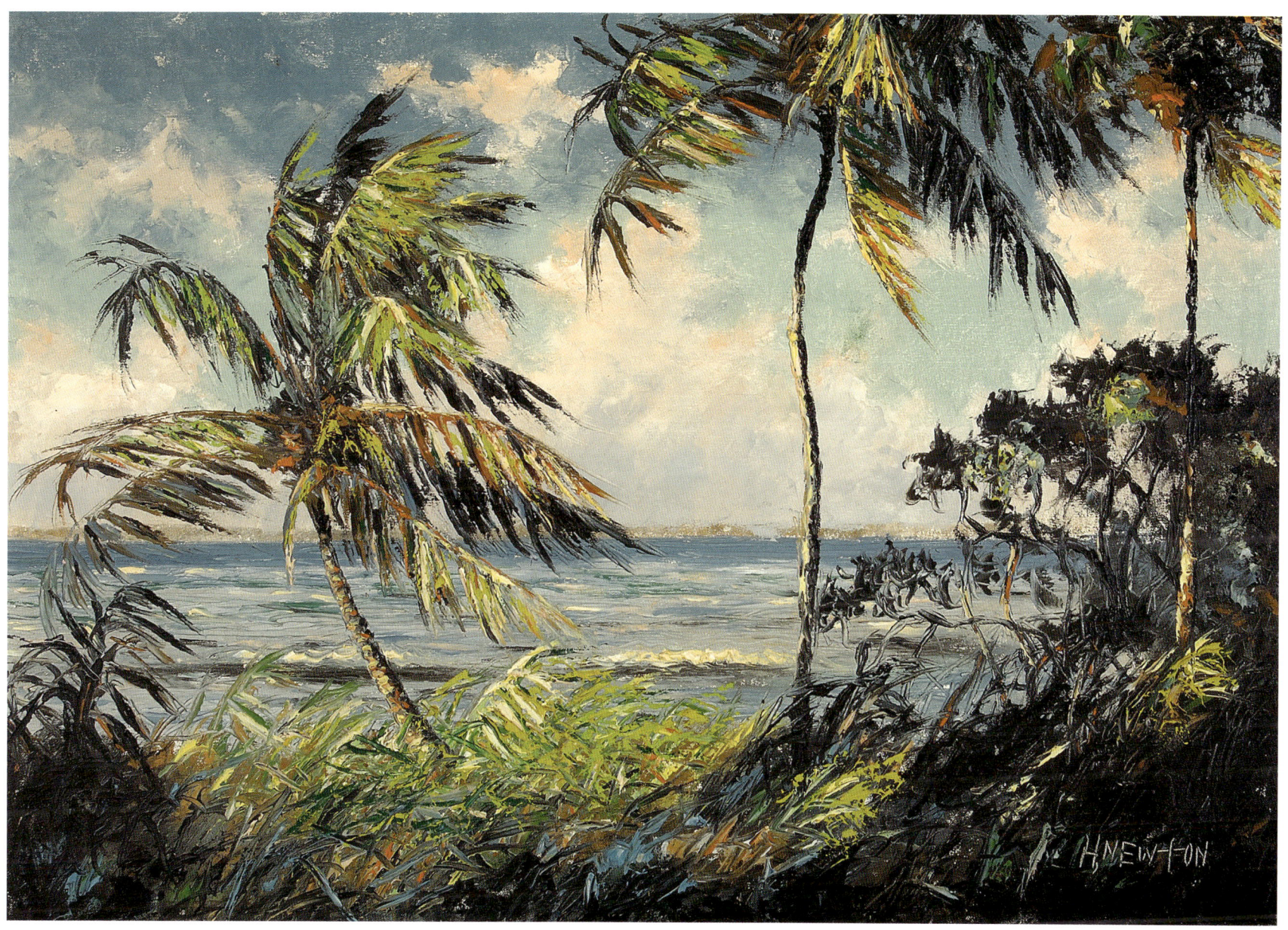

43. 19½" × 23½" oil on canvas board.

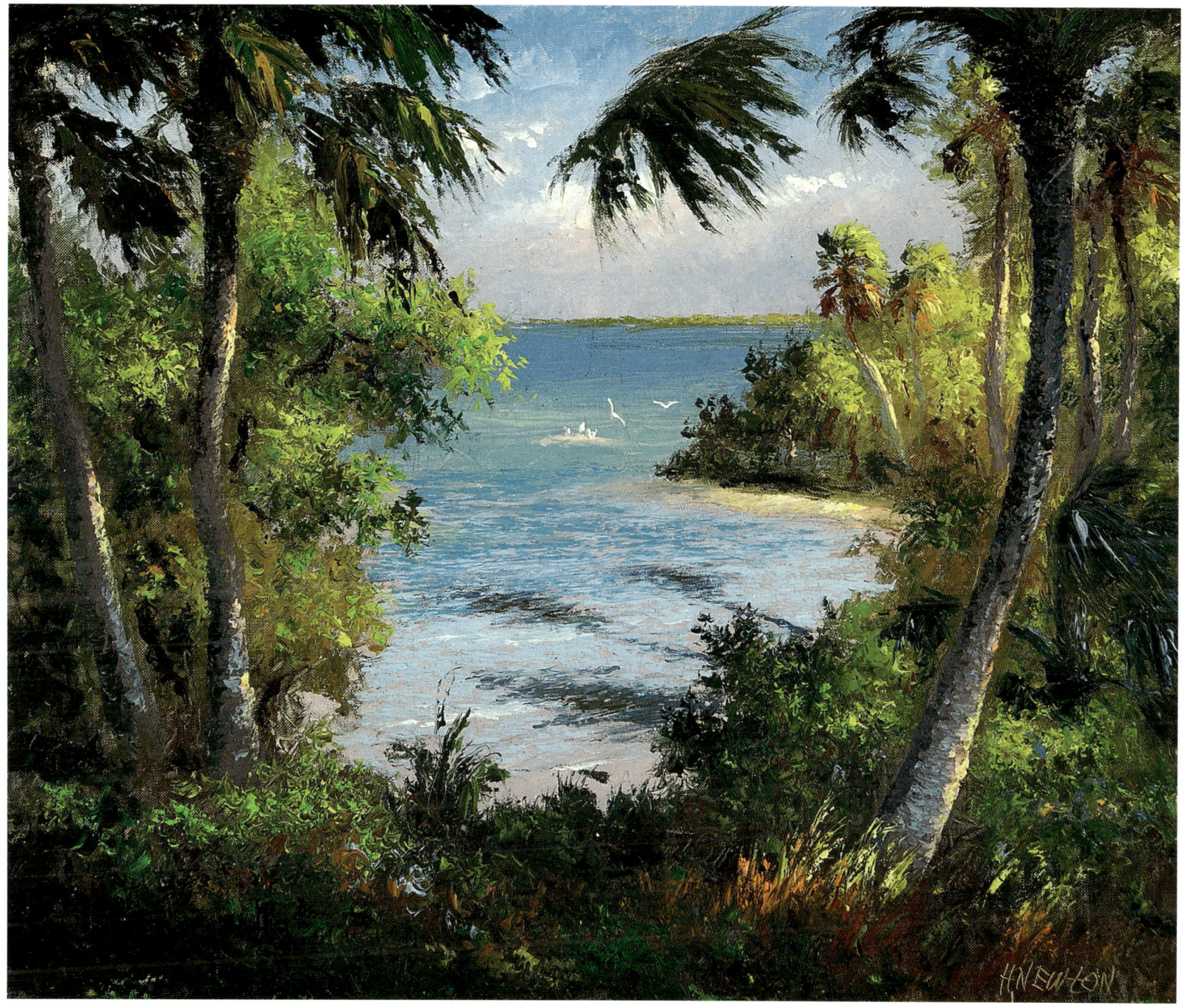

44. 23⅝" × 29½" oil on canvas board.

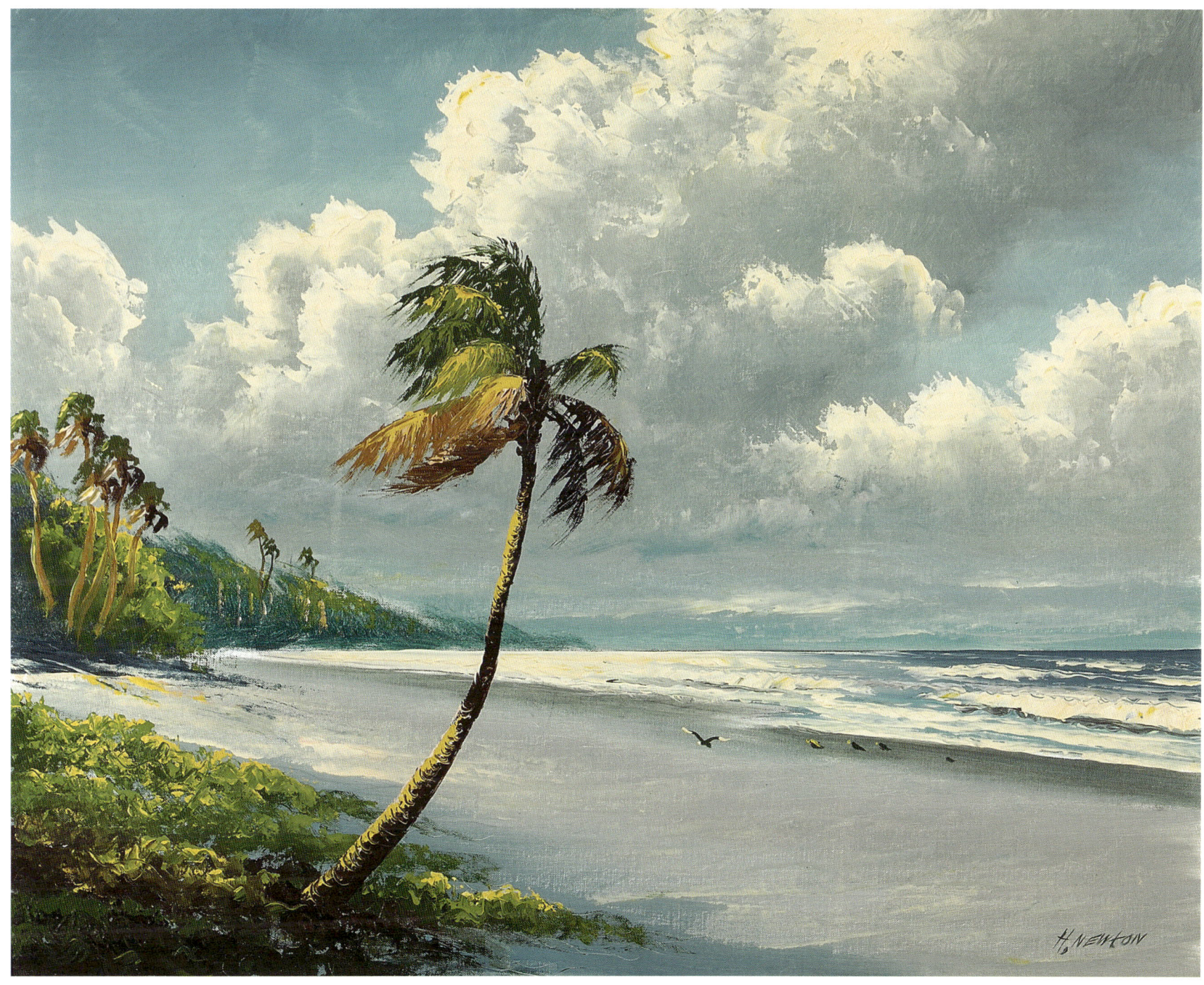

H. NEWTON

45. 23" × 47" oil on Masonite.

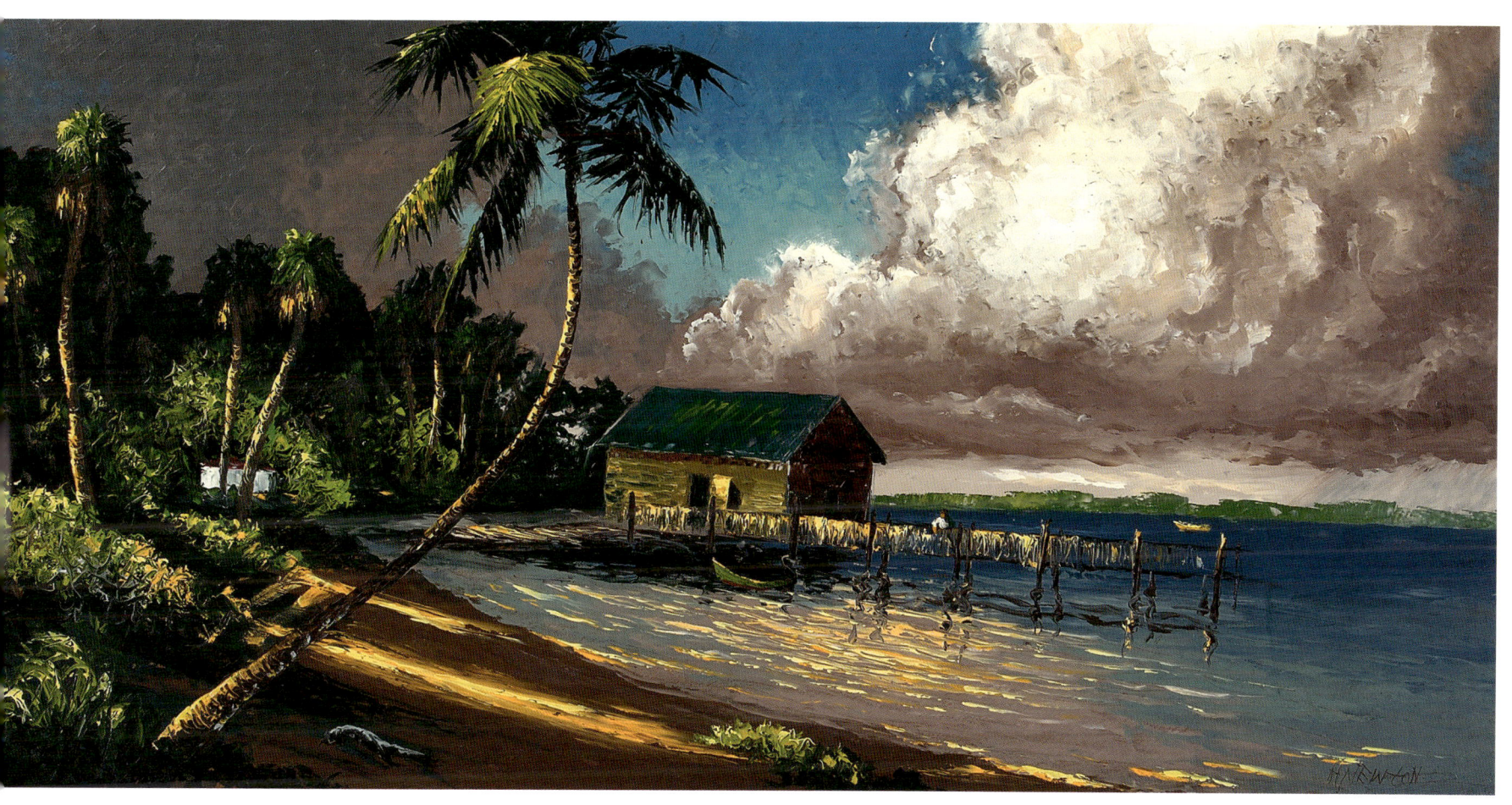

46. 23" × 47" oil on Masonite.

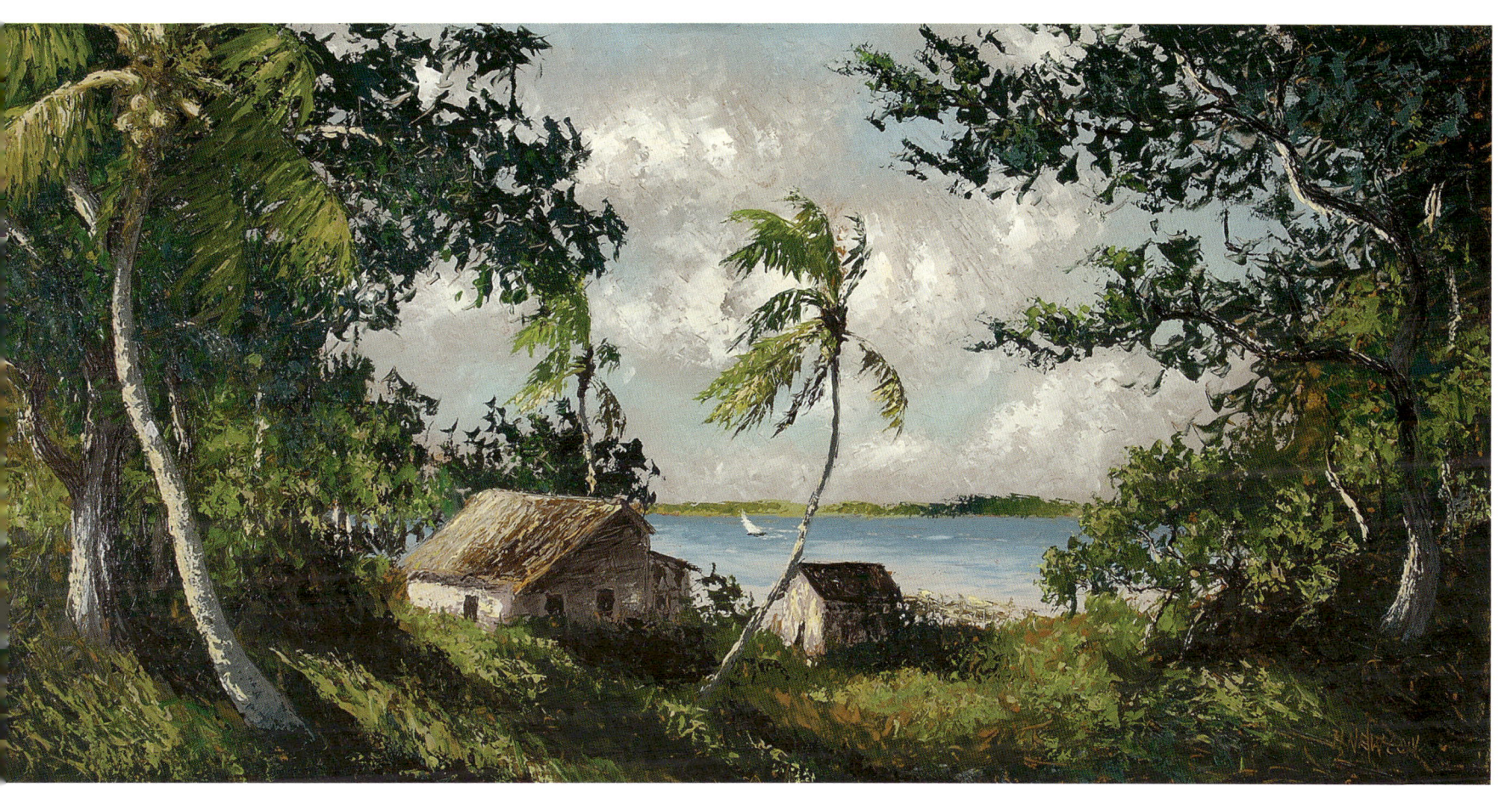

47. 23⅛" × 47⅜" oil on Masonite.

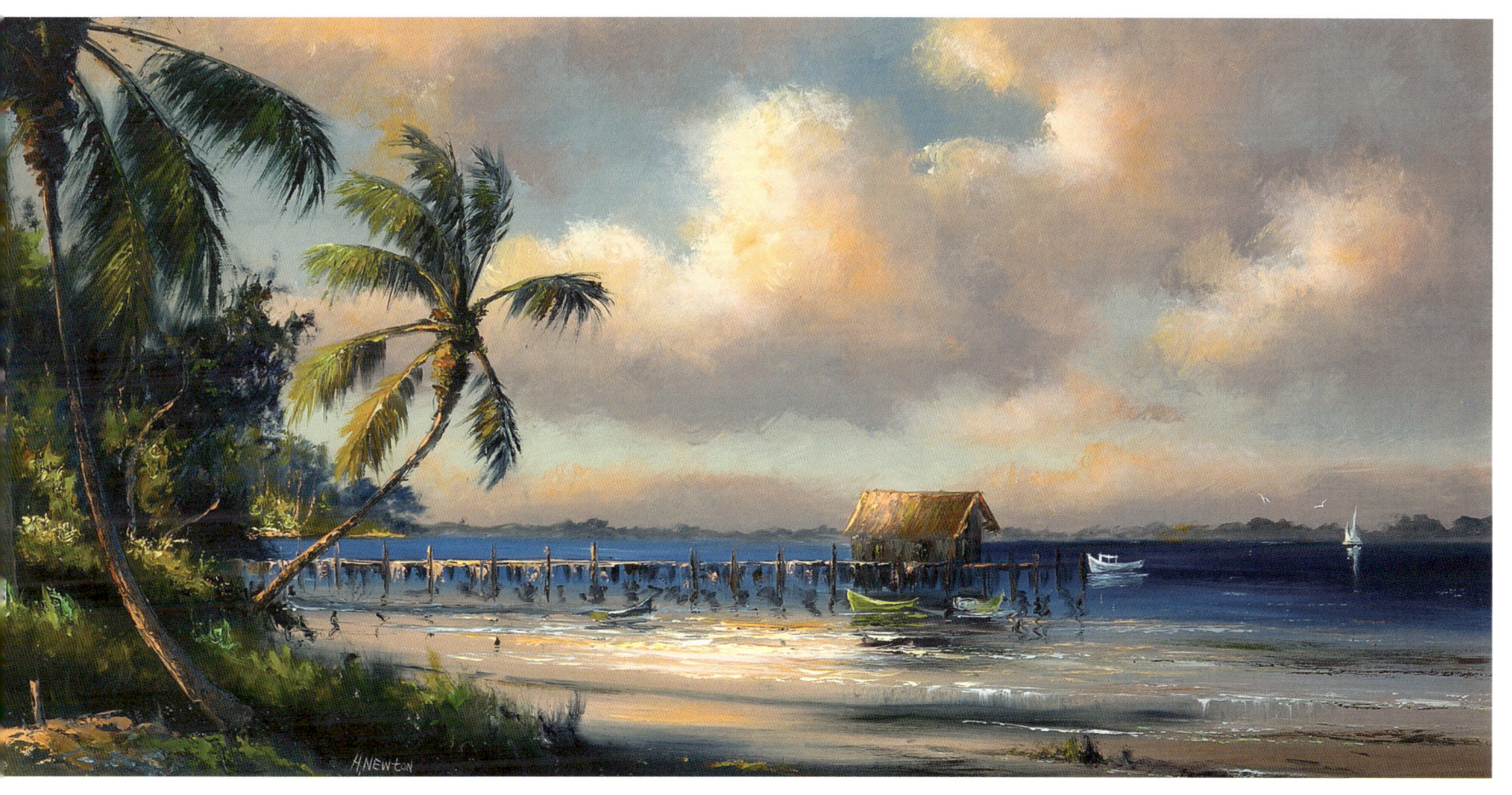

48. 19⅜" × 23⅜" oil on canvas board.

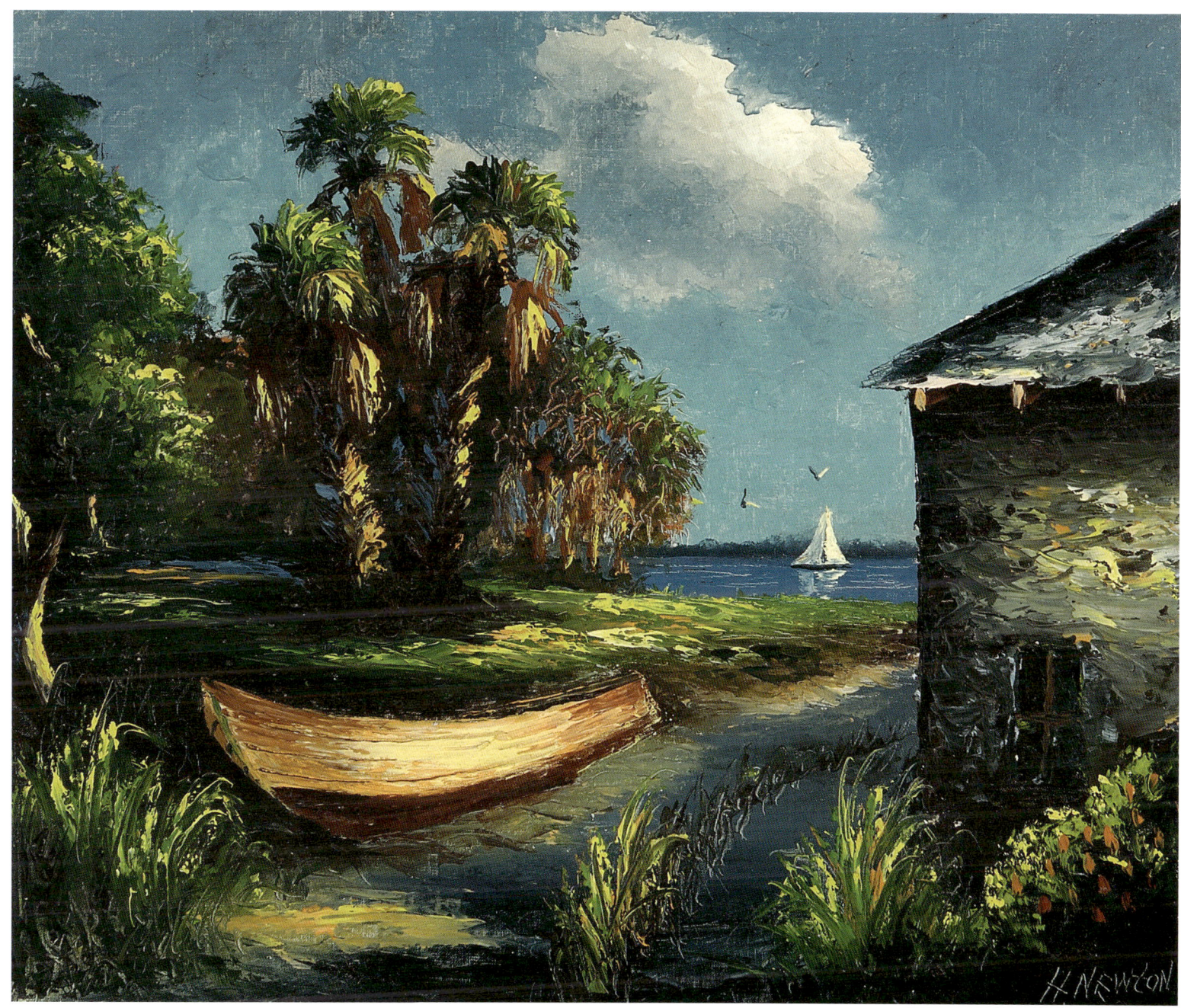

49. 23⅛" × 29⅛" oil on stretched canvas.

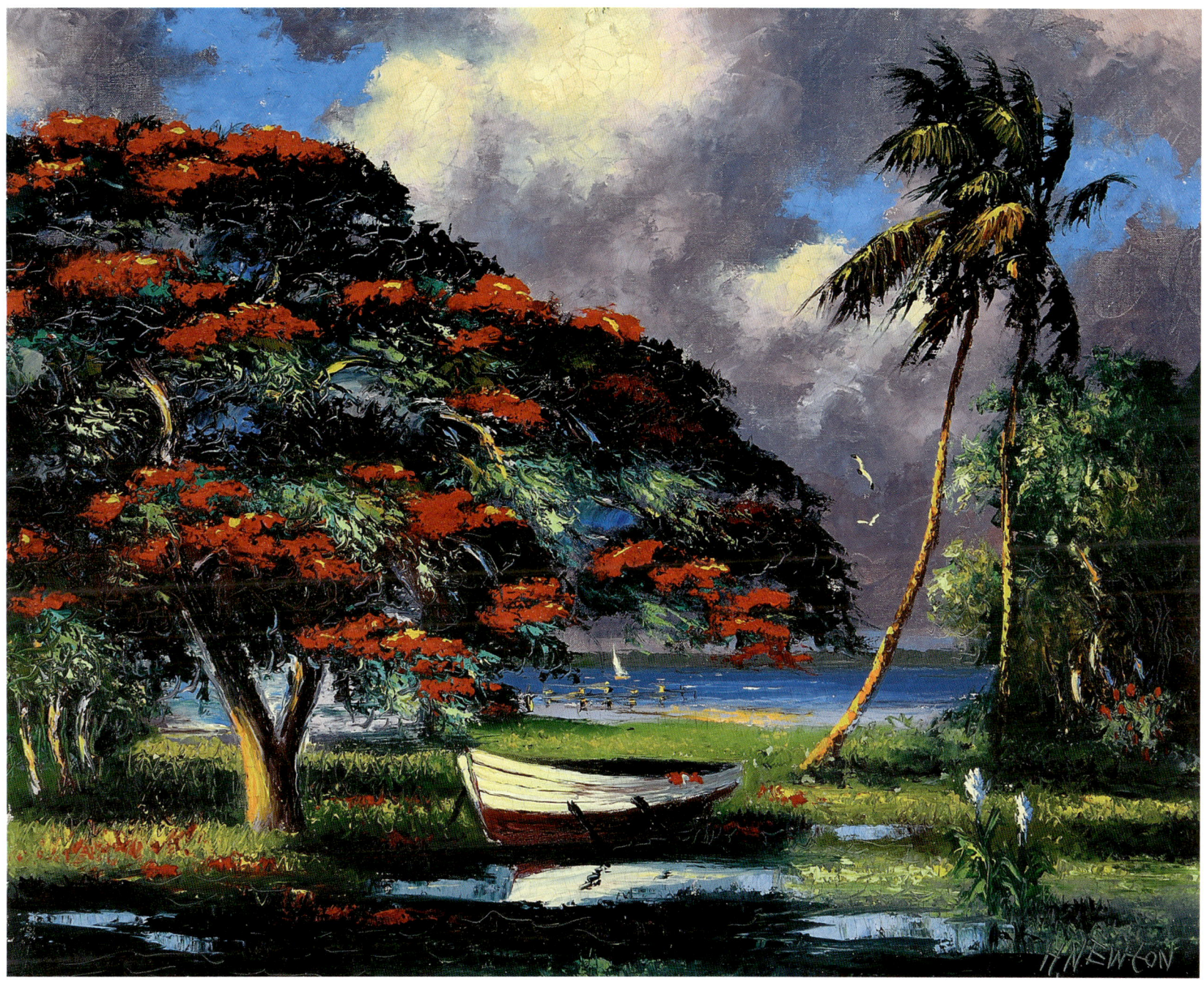

50. 17¼" × 23¼" oil on canvas board.

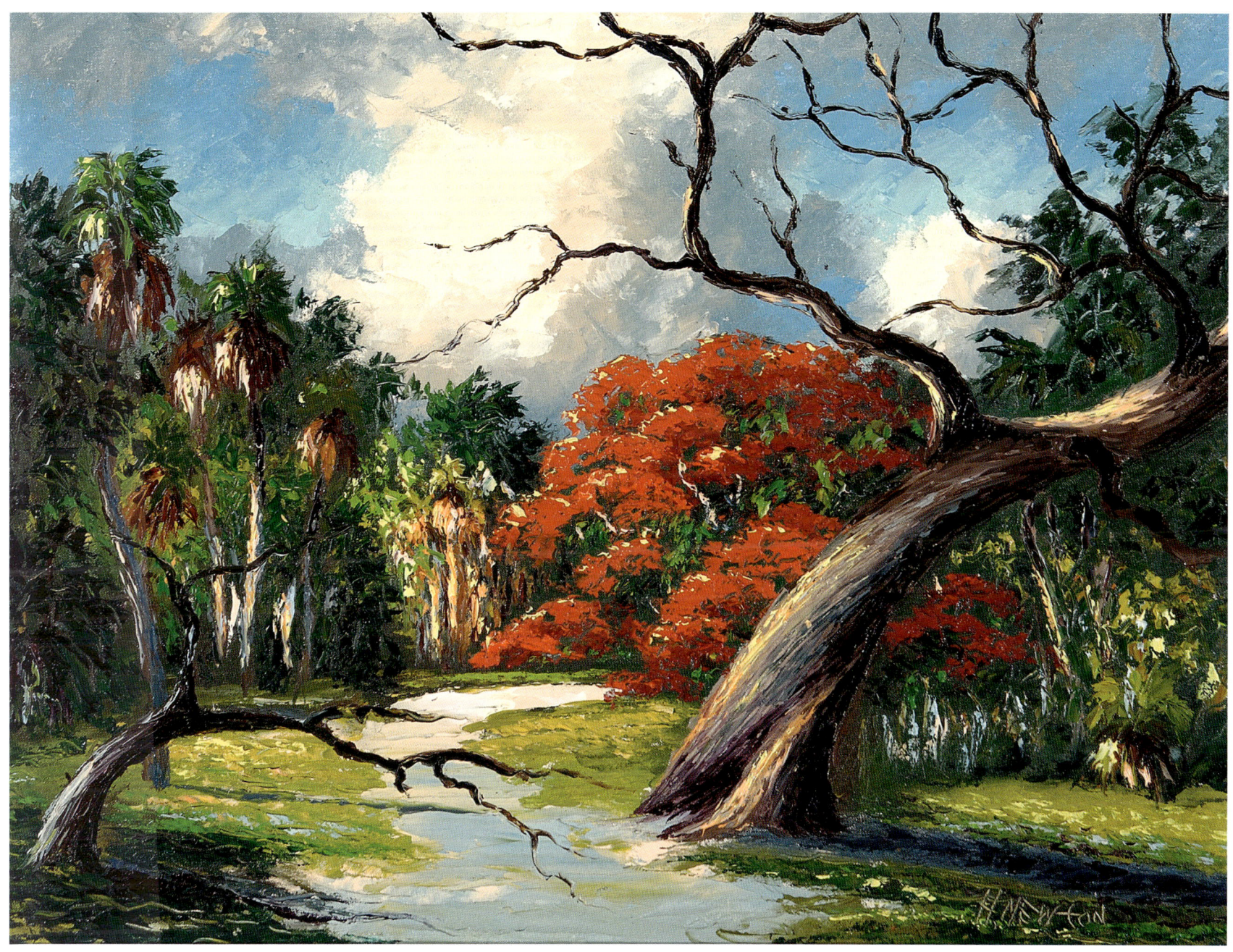

51. 23¼" × 29¼" oil on Upson board.

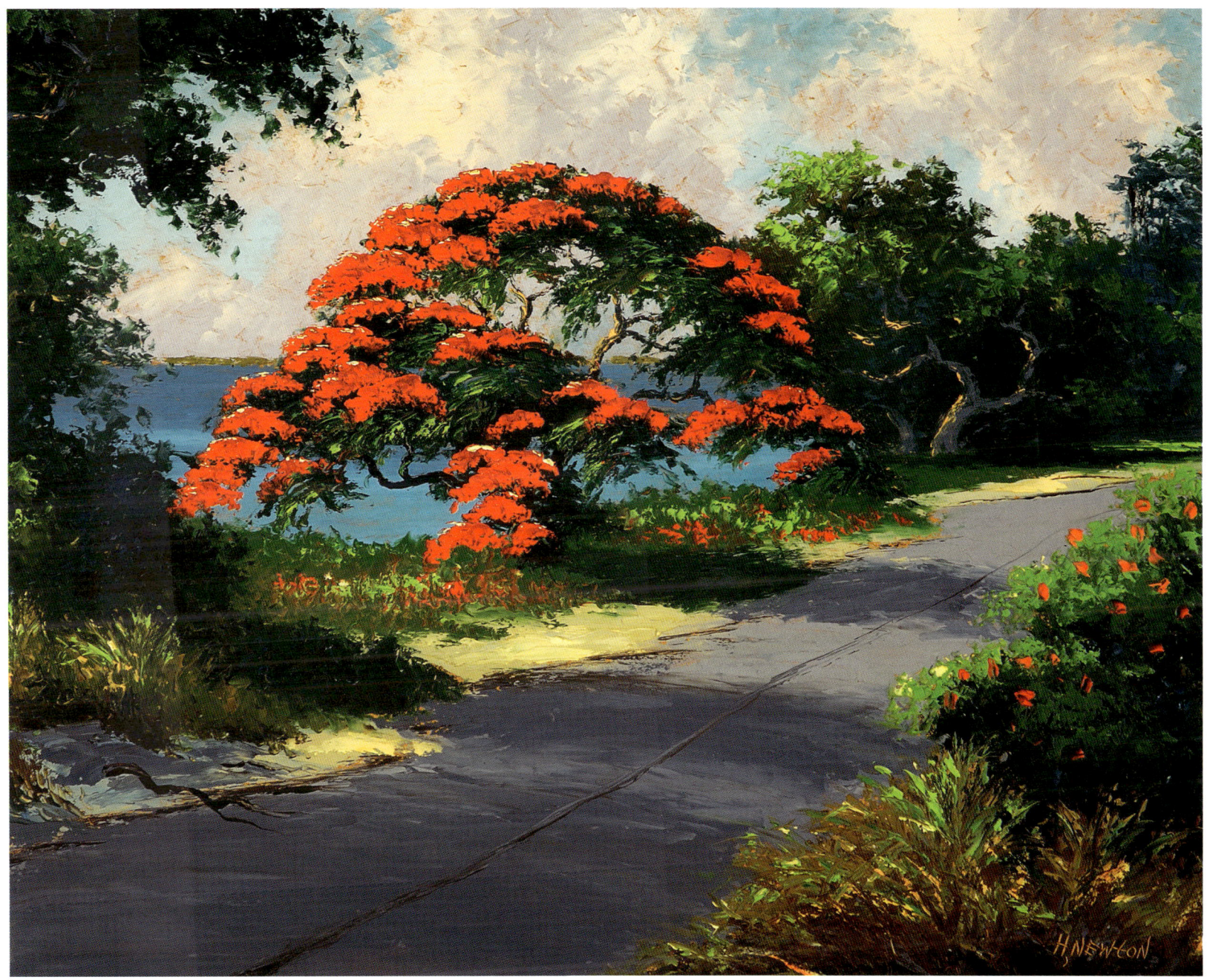

52. 19⅛″ × 39⅛″ oil on stretched canvas.

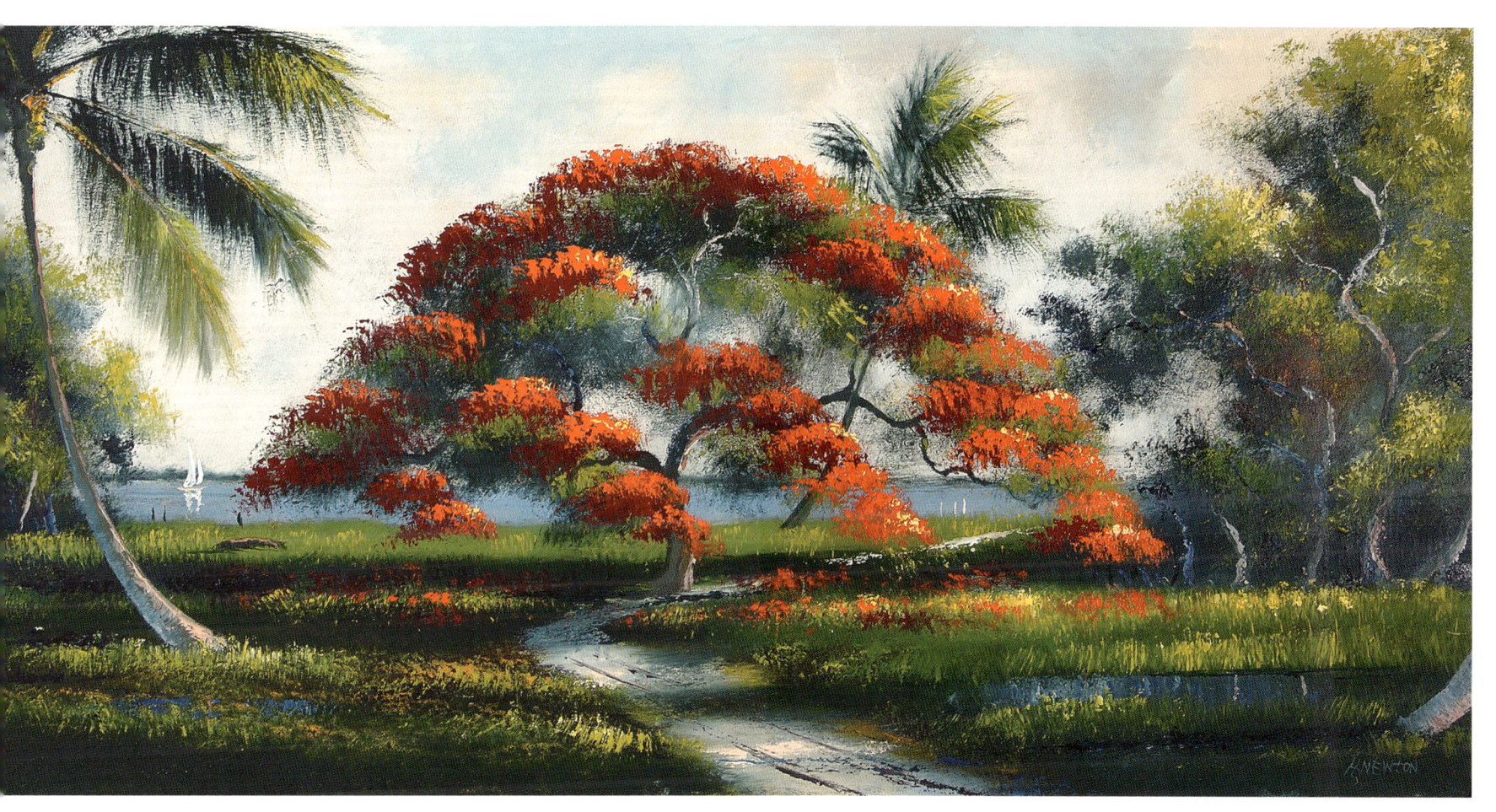

53. 23⅜" × 35⅜" oil on Upson board.

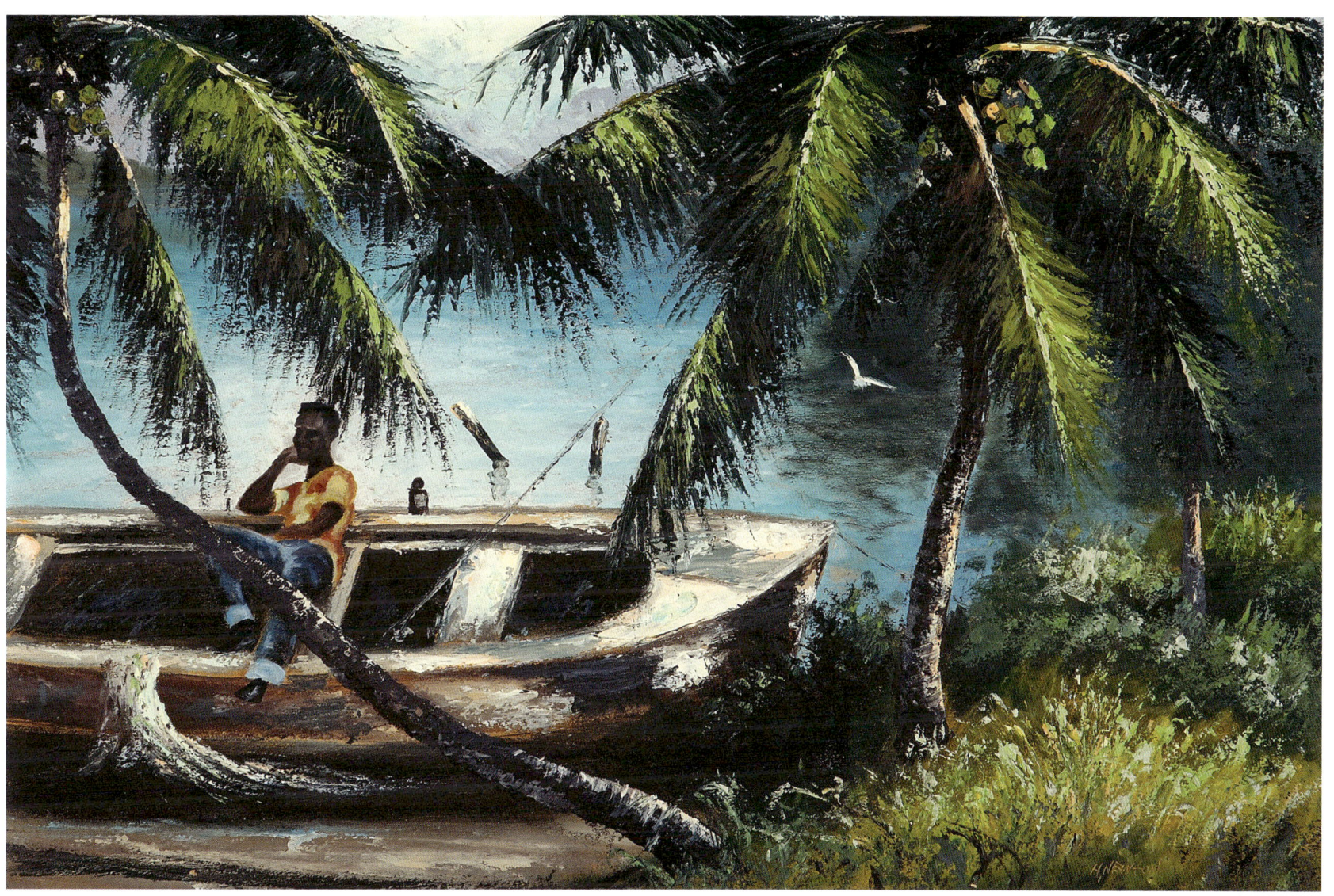

54. 23" × 29" oil on Upson board.

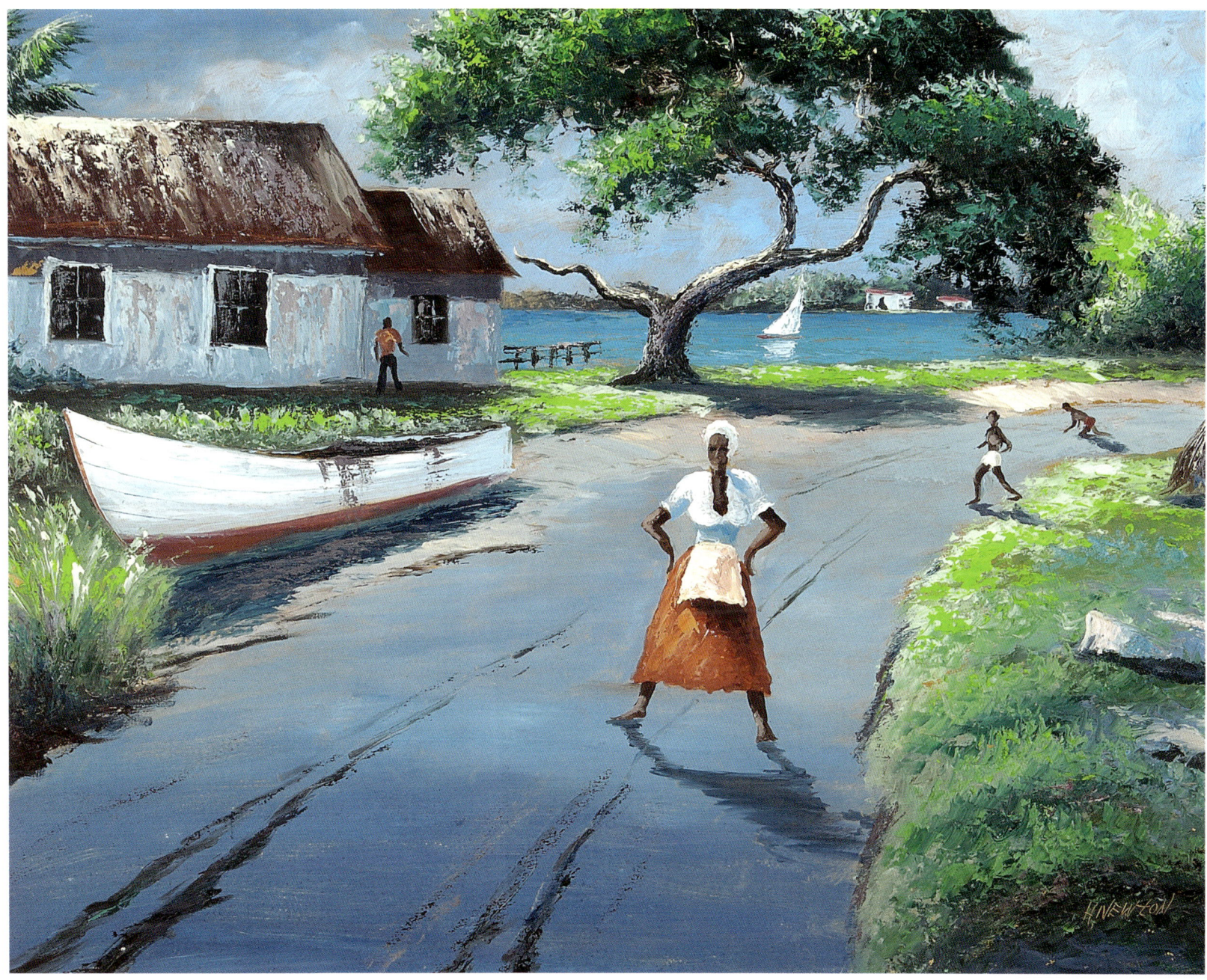

55. 17⅜" × 23¼" oil on canvas board.

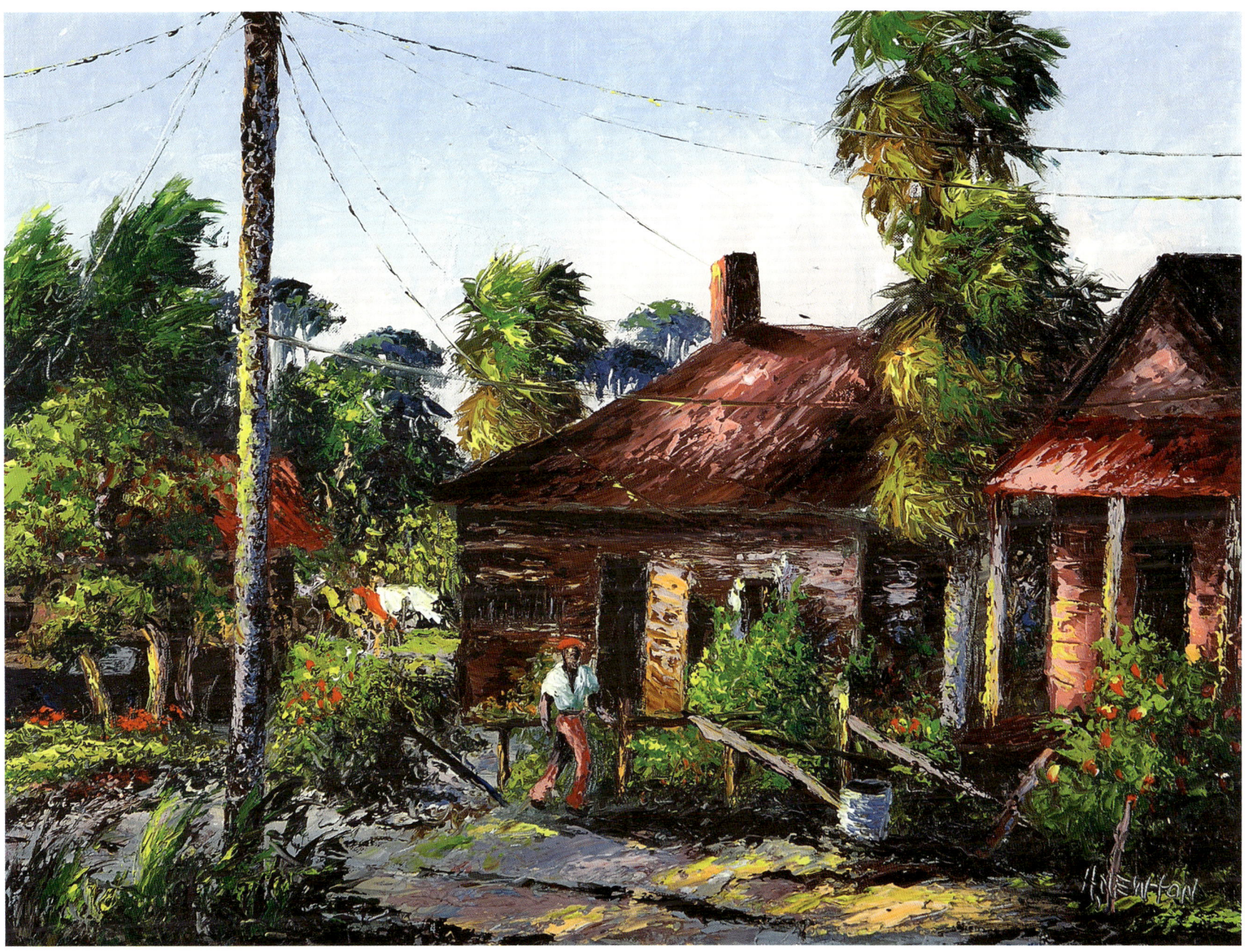

56. 23⅜" × 29⅛" oil on Upson board.

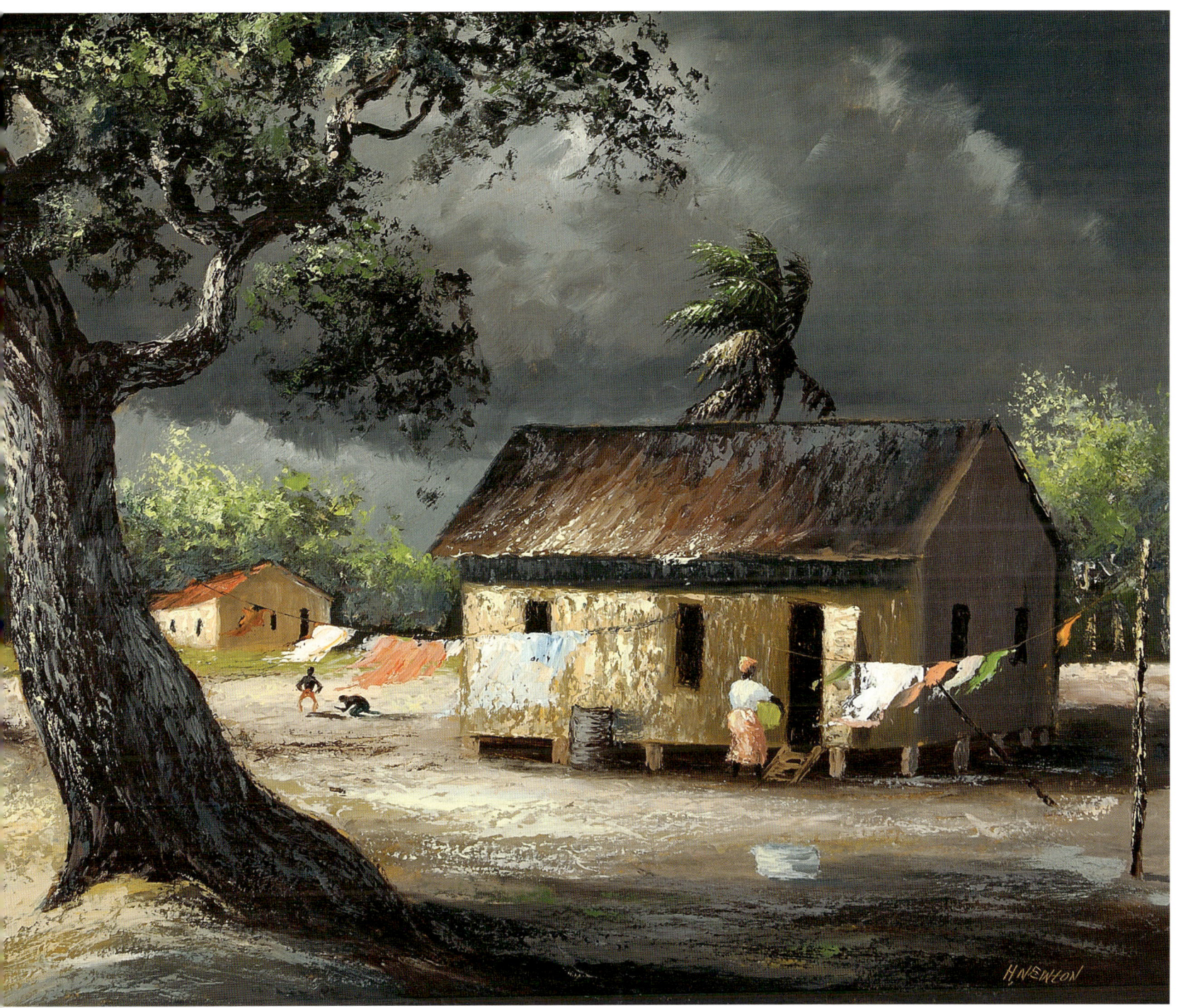

57. 26⅞" × 46⅞" oil on Upson board.

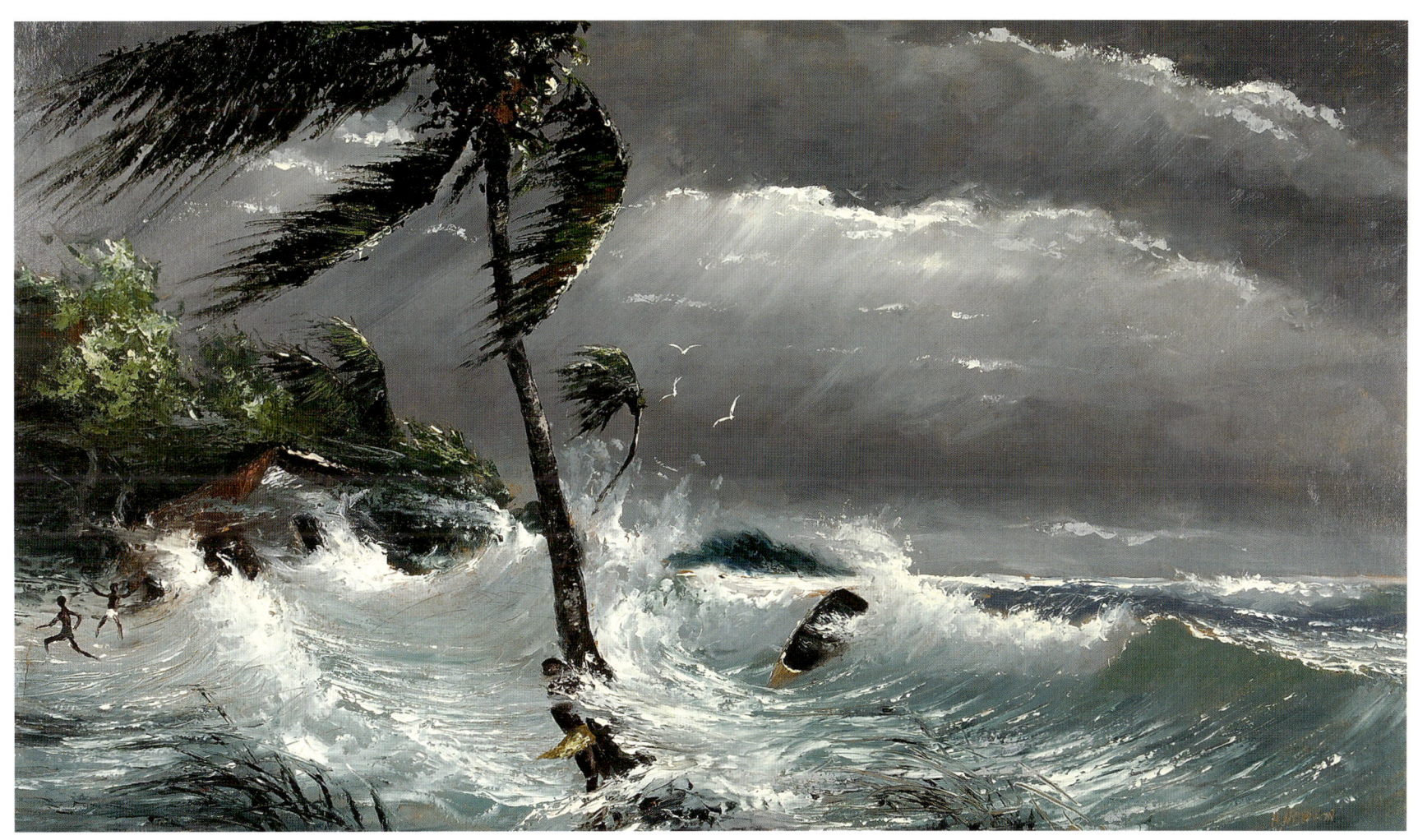

58. 23½″ × 35⅜″ oil on Masonite.

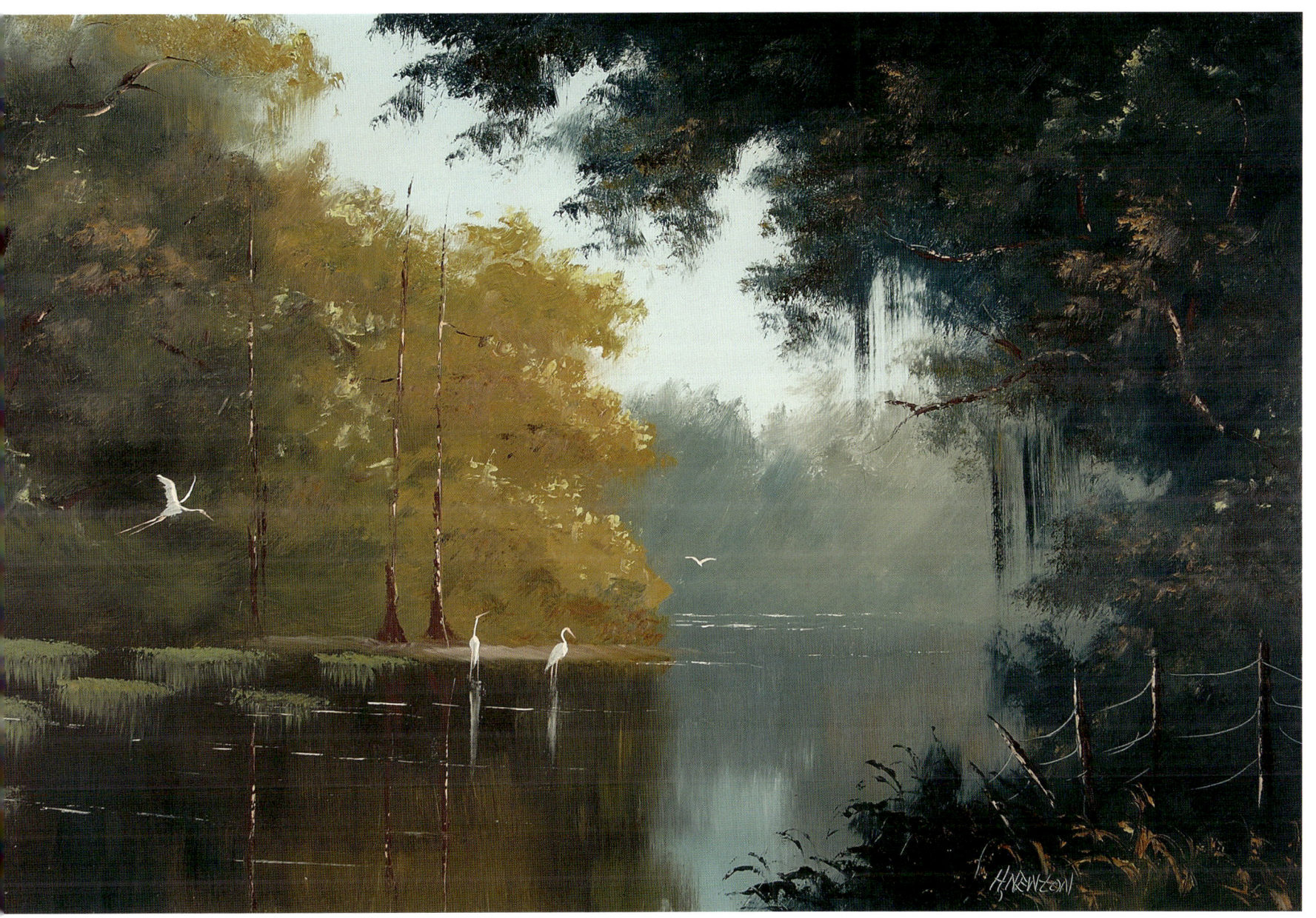

59. 13½" × 15½" oil on Masonite.

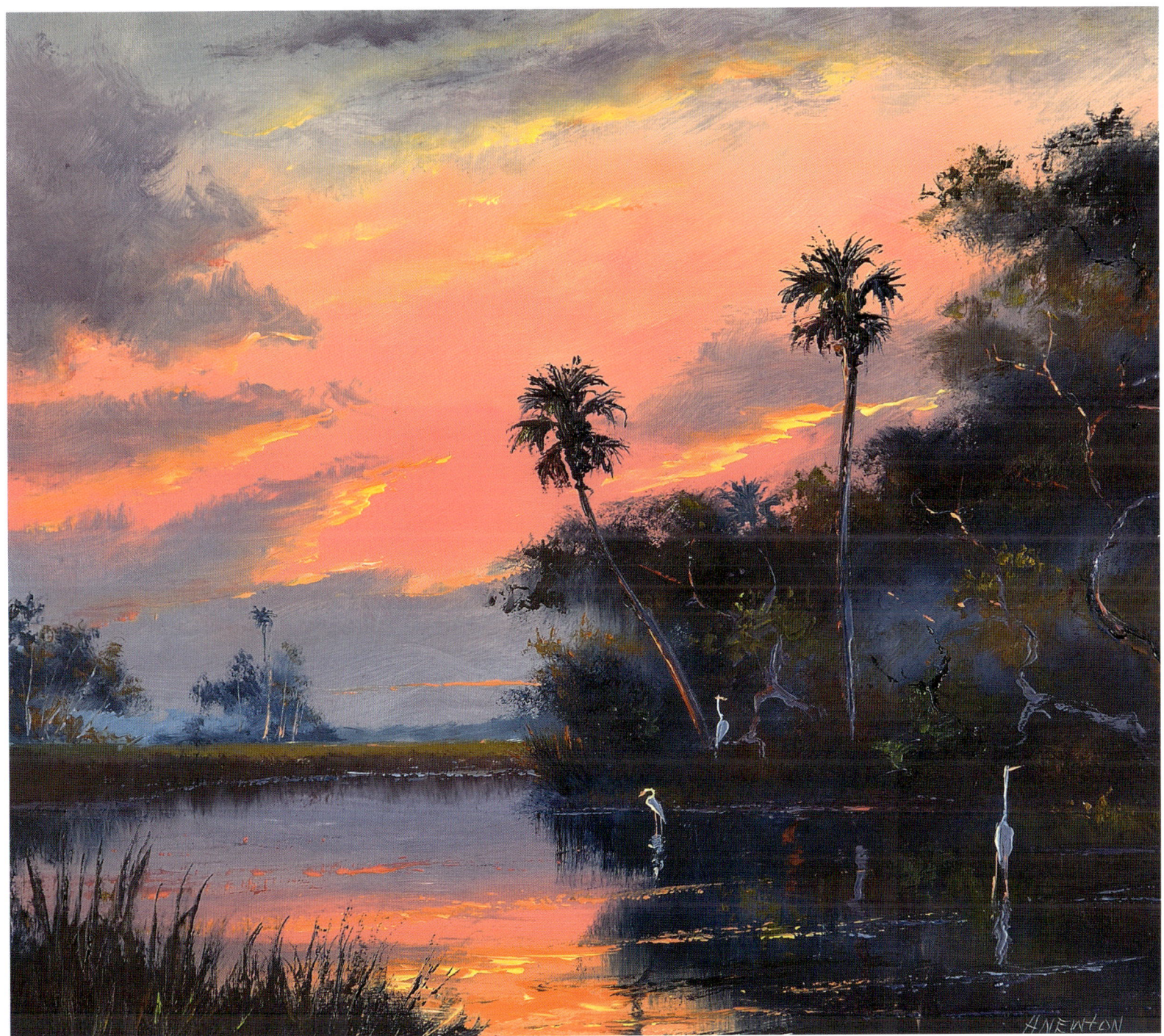

60. 22⅞" × 47⅛" oil on Masonite.

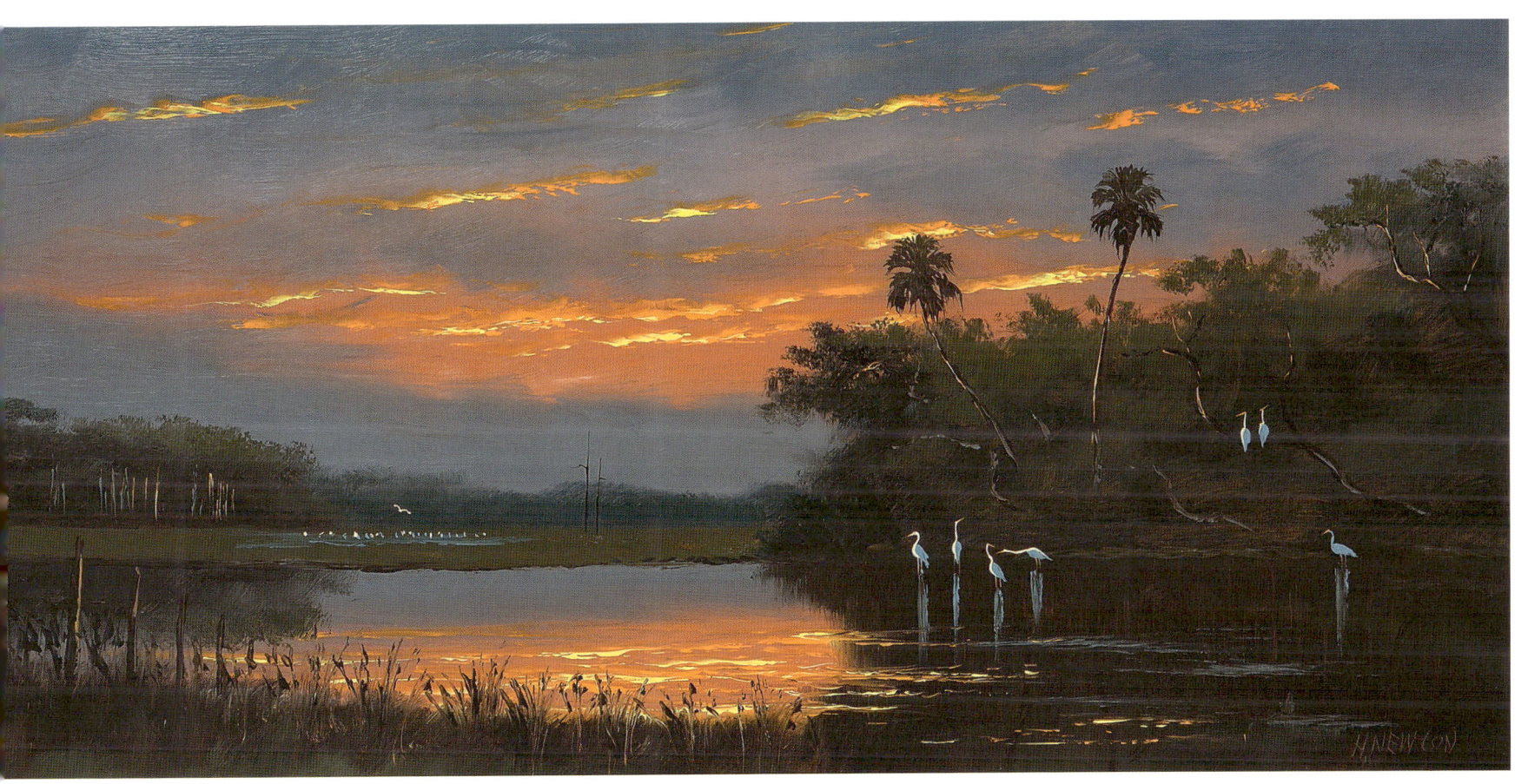

61. 23⅜" × 35" oil on Masonite.

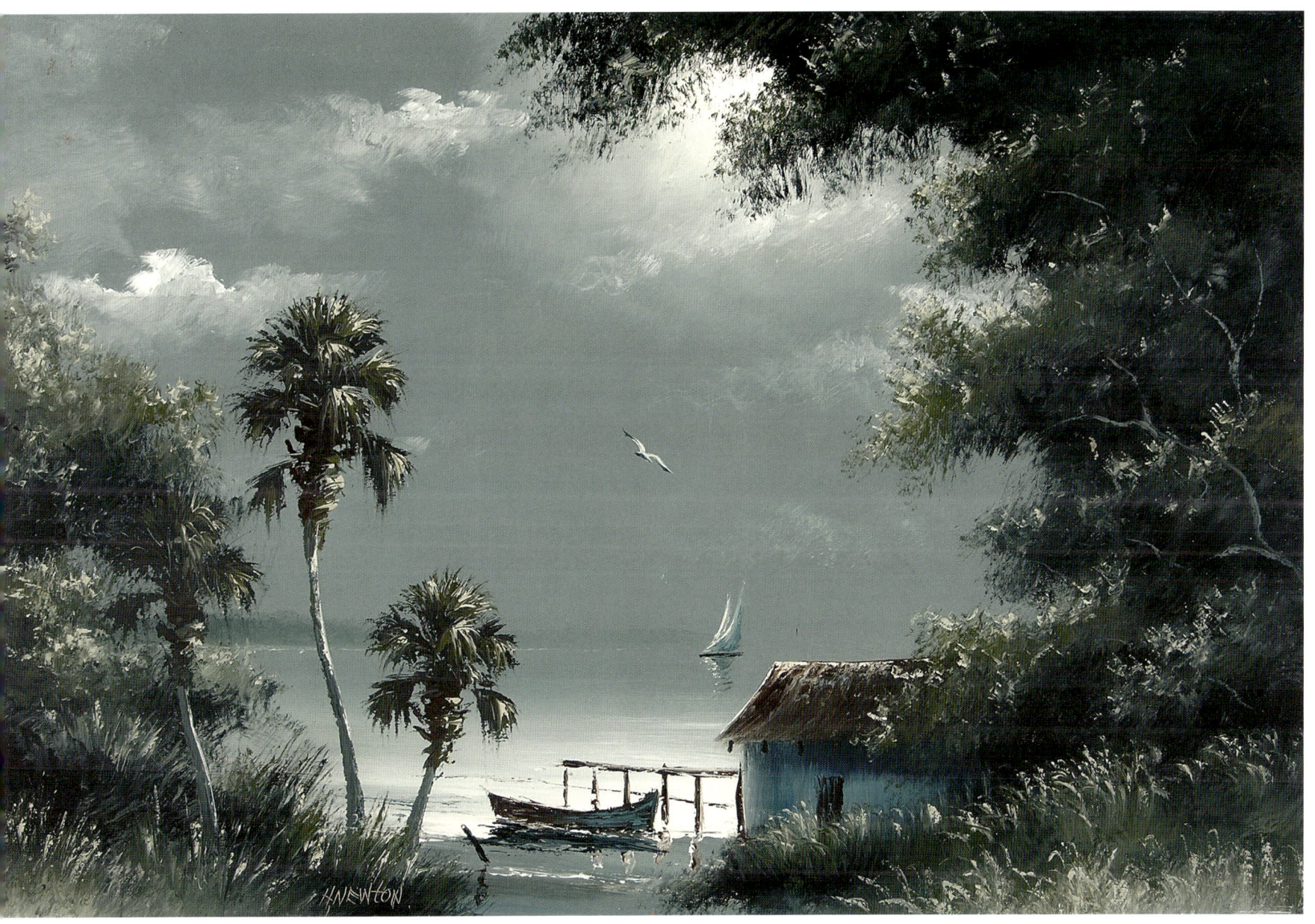

62. 23½" × 35½" oil on Upson board.

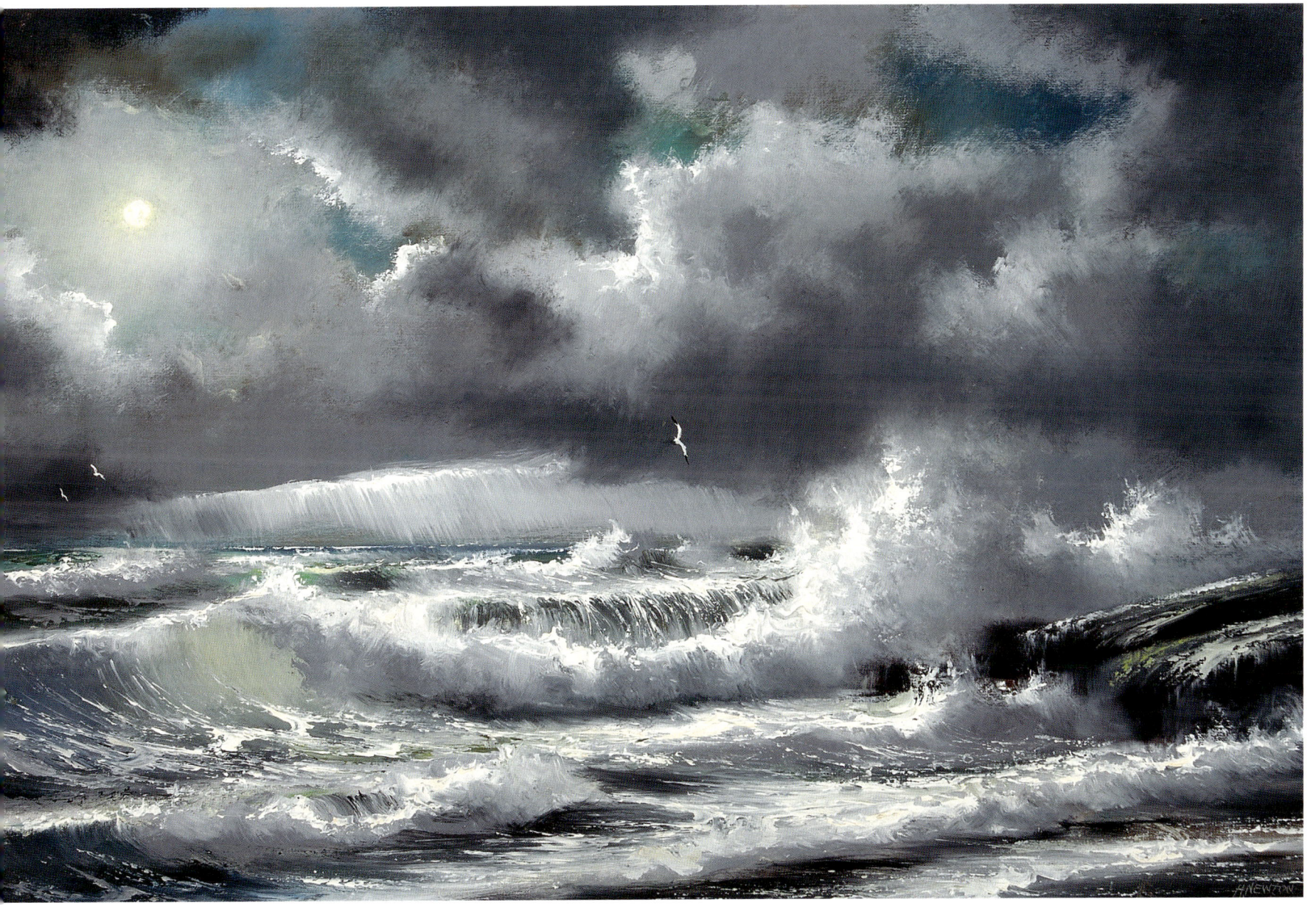

Gary Monroe, a native of Miami Beach, has photographed throughout Brazil, Israel, Cuba, India, Trinidad, Poland, and Egypt, among other international destinations. He is best known for his long-term photographic involvements with the elderly's old-world culture of South Beach, Haiti during the end of the Duvalier regime and foray into democracy, and tourism as a "rite of passage." He has received various honors and distinctions for his work, including two National Endowments for the Arts, four Florida Humanities Council Fellowships, a State of Florida arts fellowship, and two Fulbright Foundation fellowships. Monroe is the author of *The Highwaymen: Florida's African-American Landscape Painters* and three other books on Florida's Highwaymen artists. He has written nine books, most of which acknowledge unrecognized self-taught Florida artists. His most recent book, *E. G. Barnhill: Florida Photographer, Adventurer, Entrepreneur*, highlights the artist's hand-colored photographs.

Related-interest titles from University Press of Florida

The African American Heritage of Florida
Edited by David R. Colburn and Jane L. Landers

An American Beach for African Americans
Marsha Dean Phelts

Anna Madgigine Jai Kingsley: African Princess, Florida Slave, Plantation Slaveowner
Daniel L. Schafer

Before His Time: The Untold Story of Harry T. Moore, America's First Civil Rights Martyr
Ben Green

Black Miami in the Twentieth Century
Marvin Dunn

The Highwaymen: Florida's African-American Landscape Painters
Gary Monroe

A History of Visual Art in Sarasota
Pat Ringling Buck, Marcia Corbino, and Kevin Dean

Martin Johnson Heade in Florida
Roberta Smith Favis

For more information on these and other books, visit our website at www.upf.com.